CREATED EQUAL

CREATED EQUAL

▼

Faith Development and Prejudice

Robert S. Junge

Writer's Showcase
presented by *Writer's Digest*
San Jose New York Lincoln Shanghai

Created Equal
Faith Development and Prejudice

Writer's Showcase
presented by *Writer's Digest*
an imprint of iUniverse.com, Inc.

For information address:
iUniverse.com, Inc.
5220 S 16th, Ste. 200
Lincoln, NE 68512
www.iuniverse.com

ISBN: 0-595-15088-8

Printed in the United States of America

To
Vera

Acknowledgements

With particular thanks to Alaine York and Don Fitzpatrick for their help in the editing and preparation of this work.

CONTENTS

Introduction

This book wrestles with the challenge of human variety and its accompanying prejudices. It assumes that, given that variety, lasting answers to the problem of prejudice must be individual and deeply personal matters of faith. It also assumes that faith is the product of a process of human growth.

I have often been frustrated by studies that attempt to quantify the process of human growth and reduce it to statistics. It often seems that the less reliable statistically a study is, the more insightful it is in human terms. No doubt some human behavior is predictable. Some studies even seem to correlate human behavior with chemical imbalances. Others explain it in terms of submicroscopic hereditary entities whose existence we can only postulate. Such studies have done remarkable and helpful things, and I have no wish to denigrate

them. I am sure that behaviorists and
laboratory psychologists can also add
significant dimensions to our understanding
of human differences.

For example, when a waitress ignores a
black person at a country club, it may be in
part the result of conditioned behavior. When
a black person enters a room actively expect-
ing to be slighted, the behavior that follows
may in some way be predictable. But these
responses seem to me to be symptoms, not
the disease. Surely I should expect to be
laughed at if, in the fashion of Minotehka, I
were to assert that prejudice was merely a
chemical reaction.

In addition to the studies of the behaviorists, the combined experience of lifetimes of
counseling and observation has produced a
wealth of helpful techniques for facilitating
human interaction. The analysts reach to levels of human response that add a dimension
to the more precise predictions and controls
of the laboratory. Many schools of psychology
have contributed valuable insights into our
ability simply to get along. Thousands of people are deeply grateful for this dedicated
work, which has significantly changed their
lives. Surely this work too must be respected.
Some of the incidents described in this book
might be probed by the analysts, and the origin of prejudice might be more sharply
defined in the process.

Still, even the experts are unable to keep up with all the data that is being generated. They cannot master the wide-ranging theories of interpretation which appear in journal after journal. Therefore, in their work many focus on one or two schools of thought, while others are more eclectic, taking a little of the "best" from here and there. Many practitioners simply try to prevent the circuits from going out on overload and to keep the connections functioning in the complex networks of human relationships. They help us deal with each other in our minute-to-minute encounters in a rushing world. But their very ethics prevent them from wrestling with prejudicial relationships at the values level. Their "solutions" end up being only relative to the circumstance at hand and do not resolve the human dilemma of created difference itself.

We who are outside these fields are somehow intimidated by all this expertise. When confronted with significant issues such as prejudice, we can feel utterly inadequate without all this knowledge. Yet we are concerned, and daily life demands response. From somewhere deep within us we know that what we do and say can make some difference. So partly on the basis of experience and partly on the basis of our religious values, we develop simpler and more manageable convictions. We feel driven to find a way to deal with the complexity of human behavior in simple terms of right and wrong. Life won't let us merely react. We make conscious decisions on the basis of what we know and believe is right.

When confronted with prejudice then, most of us, at least in our better moments, turn to both our experience and our religious convictions. We recognize that what we believe and feel is on a different level from what we do and say, and yet those beliefs and feelings influence and often control our words and deeds. Despite the claims that we are the products of our environment, we feel free and responsible for our lives and how they unfold. At our happiest and best, we are not driven but in the driver's seat.

Religion defines the meaning of life, particularly our inner life of thought and affection. From religion we reflect upon experience, but refuse to accept the idea that we are simply the unthinking products of that experience. The simple fact, which I hope to illustrate through my experience, is that religion can answer such challenges as human prejudice, can guide our thoughts, and can lead our affections. If it cannot, how can it be our religion? Prejudice builds up one thought and one affection at a time. The challenges it presents must be met with answers we can live with and live by.

Many have observed that the mind grows by stages. So too does religious conscience.

The prior stage must take root, blossom, and produce its fruit to provide the basis for the next stage. In part, growth is powered by a positive thrust, a creative drive to become human. But we often acquire the fruits of growth through being challenged. The tree of our emerging life requires pruning as it goes from season to season. So we can say that as conscience grows, so do the challenges to it.

One such challenge is coping with human variety, step-by-step as we go through stages of human development. Prejudice between races, cultures, and sexes emerges over and over. We hope to look at the stage-by-stage development of prejudice and at the same time point to its interior antidote, i.e. the stage-by-stage development of conscience.

As a teacher of developmental psychology for many years, I hope that what follows will reflect the stages of human development for the reader in such a way as to inspire continuing spiritual growth. James Fowler, particularly, has pioneered some wonderful lines of thought in this area. Piaget, Kohlberg, Erikson and many others have made significant contributions to the field. While this material is in my background, I make no pretense to precise scientific sociology, psychology, or theology. Prejudice is a problem. Let us consider it together, in the dynamic terms of human development.

As a minister of the New Church (Swedenborgian), I must admit that what follows naturally shows the influence of that church's teachings on my life. I have attempted, however, not to be doctrinaire or dogmatic. Each of us has a responsibility to our own God as we from conscience see Him. I hope that nothing said here will in any way violate that individual freedom or that personal responsibility.

In an effort to trace and illustrate the stages of growth, I have looked back on the development of my own personal prejudices. My hope is that these reflections will not be seen as an old man's confessions, but will instead encourage the reader to seek out the origins and the progressive stages in the development of his own prejudices and then reflect on what he can do to overcome them in himself and in his world.

My work as a church administrator has given me a wonderful opportunity to work on deeply human concerns with friends in Africa, South America, Europe, and the Orient, as well as here in North America. To give background and a sense of reality, I have included descriptions of some of these experiences.

We are not all faced with the challenge of dealing with different races or cultures in day-to-day life, but we are all faced with the difference between men and women. The challenge of defining and handling the difference between the two sexes has erupted in the world during my years as a pastor. I include some of my experiences in my own marriage and in my pastoral counseling to try to enlarge the picture I present. I believe it is no accident that we find ourselves struggling with sex difference at the same time as we confront racial and cultural differences. Sex difference is included here to demonstrate that the development of faith itself is the answer to dealing with all forms of diversity and not simply a way of looking at the single problem of racial prejudice. I also reflect on marriage because in the sphere of love for our partners, God gives us the easiest setting possible for learning the harmony of two so completely different beings. What is more, marriage and family play key roles in meeting and answering prejudice.

The bottom line is that we all need to make decisions in our own day-to-day lives. We cannot always depend upon experts. In some areas of life only God is the Expert. We can depend upon Him even if we do not fully understand Him. If our present answers are inadequate, surely we can learn from reflecting upon our past experience and from looking honestly at our beliefs about right and wrong.

At whatever stage in life we are, with whatever level of beliefs we bring to the problem of prejudice, I pray that each reader will reflect deeply and then ask, "What does my God want me to do?" If we bring all that we can to the problem of handling human variety, there will be change. We will acquire the tools to make a difference. If we learn to serve the One in whose image we were created, humanity itself will surely grow through our individual consciences. Out of the very differences He created, God can compose and conduct a Divine symphony in genuine and universal terms.

From its roots in creation itself, human variety will surely affect us. We will have to respond to it in some form. Our response should be a thoughtful choice using every religious and scientific resource we have at the time. We owe that to our humanity.

The goal of the book is to present these challenges:

Think about your life. Compare your prejudices and your convictions. Ask, "What does my God want me to do?" Then do it.

I

▼

PRECIOUS BEGINNINGS
BONDING AND INTUITIVE TRUST

In September 1929, in a small Midwestern town, there was an "accident." In a tubular steel bed with coil springs and a lumpy cotton mattress, the rhythm method failed, and I was conceived. The doctors had said that another pregnancy might take my mother's life. With a daughter and two sons already, my father must surely have wondered more than once what he would do if those awesome predictions came true.

When the stock market crashed a month later, my father lost his job and remained unemployed for some seven years. How often he must have asked "Why?" I'm sure that in many subtle ways the "accident" of my birth influenced his later reactions to me. But neither he nor my mother regarded it as truly accidental. Rather, to them it was something that happened within an all-wise Providence. Their religious faith and conscience significantly modified a potential source of prejudice. Perhaps they knew that the fundamental answer to all forms of prejudice is a mature religious conscience, for just as prejudice can grow throughout life, so its antidote, conscience, can be laid up layer upon layer to combat it.

Those months of waiting filled my parents with anxious concern. Yet they found courage too, not by trusting in the frailties of this world, but in the God-given potential of human life itself. Such trust in the idea that all of us, despite our differences, have a Divine origin is a key to accepting those differences—the beginning of the antidote.

From the start, I differed from 50% of the population. I was a male. And though my family had been in America for several generations, my heredity was almost entirely German. (My grandparents still spoke it when they didn't want us to know what they were talking about.) My white skin set me apart from many other babies in the city hospital nursery where my Mom went for special natal care. My bright blue eyes easily marked me as different from those with dark eyes. Barring undernourishment, my genes called for an eventual height of six feet. I was country, not city. As a depression baby, poor, not rich. Even from among all the babies in the hospital nursery you could pick me out.

God made me different. That was a "given." I came to know it, to accept it, and even to be proud of it. If I had not, I would be in no position to accept others for their "givens," their variety.

We usually respond to variety in nature with great delight. Look at a day lily etched in orange against a green lawn. Consider the tight clusters of yellow mums beside it. Compare either of them to the long lavender triangles that grace the butterfly bush as it rises with the others in the same garden. We appreciate the contrasts of the flowers. We even unwind a few notches mentally as we breathe in the blend of their gentle scents.

In another place, what a wonder to see the Colorado blue spruce behind the golden leaves of the aspen on a fall day. Both seem to need each other under that incomparable blue sky. And the drifting clouds seem to have been created just to enhance the contrasts and the wonder of the scene.

Men too differ, not just as to the sex, race, nation, or culture of their birth. Each of them has a unique set of experiences in sharp contrast to that of their fellows. Yet do they unwind and enjoy sensing those differences?

Do they wonder at those created contrasts and in them discover a magnetic need for each other? Or do those differences trigger doubt and distrust?

Difference among humans, as in nature, is created by God. Of itself it cannot be the origin of prejudice. How you and I handle that difference is. The fact is that God saw everything that He had made, and it was "very good." It is "very good" that there are blacks; it is "very good" that there are whites; it is "very good" that there are browns; and it is very good that there are males and females in all the races. It may take a lifetime to learn to accept the variety of human goodness in others as we interact with them, but surely it is God's will that we should.

Humanity itself is interactive. Since I was an "accident," my parents had a different reaction to me. I in turn had a different reaction to them. Not only did I react to their specific words and actions, but almost intuitively I also read supposed meanings into them and reacted accordingly. But establishing a useful interactive relationship with others who by definition are different from us is enormously complex. We respond not just on the level of experience, but psychologically and spiritually as well.

In the deepest sense, our relationship to God has a profound influence on the way we respond to others. Their relationship to God makes the reverse true as well. God grows on us both here and hereafter. To relate to God and to our fellow man is our uniquely human homework in the school of life.

*   *   *

Of course I cannot consciously remember the first closeness of my mother—the secure warmth of her arms, the sense of trust that must have been there and still is there. She was the first person I needed. She inspired my first love for others. I counted on her.

Those warm currents which precede conscious memory have a profound influence on our humanity. Who can sit across a room and watch a mother, Madonna-like, nursing her baby, without sensing something tender and precious? Such bonding is two-dimensional. It has both breadth and depth. Its closeness and security have a profound effect on the depth of our nascent ability to love. Its repeated warmth comforts us and weaves a broad sense of security—a confidence that can allow us to face new and different circumstances without fear.

Every one of us needs those deep affectional currents in our lives, so we all receive them. Some receive more, some less. Some receive them more and some less profoundly, but we all receive them. In the beginning these deep intuitive feelings are undifferentiated. But they very quickly focus. In almost no time we respond in a special way to our mothers.

As I reflect on my own infancy I contrast it to that of others I've observed around the world. I have walked the dusty, pock-ridden streets of a South African township. As an old woman hurries, in response to an urgent call speedily transmitted along the grapevine, I imagine her destination as a tin-roofed hut. There, her wrinkled and leathery hands will assist as God grants the birth of a new human life. As I have seen so many do, the newborn child will eagerly snuggle for nourishment. Perhaps the mother will rhythmically rock back and forth, her beautiful contralto stroking a soft melody as she gently fondles the still-wet gift in her arms. I hope the Divine presence in that moment will soften her concerns for the future. She will look down at the forehead bobbing slightly at her breast and she will smile wistfully in love. Deep inside, powerful responsive affections will warm the tiny spirit, for love is responsive. The first tender chords of ability to love are sounding ever so softly in that tiny heart.

Bonding is here. Trust is here. Love is here, even as it was there at my birth and yours.

Nearer home years ago, my sister, who served as a visiting nurse, described one incident. Amid broken bottles, beside an overturned garbage can, with discarded papers blowing around her, she ran toward a door in a dirty brick wall in a Chicago slum. She was aware of a big, slightly graying black man gliding along behind her. He identified with her mission. She recognized him as her self-appointed watchdog. With him there, no one would dare harm her.

As she entered, she turned to a child and asked for newspapers, for she had been taught that they are among the few sterile things in such a house. When the tiny voice announced its owner's entry into the world, a smile slipped over the mother's sweaty cheeks. She asked for the baby and held him close. No supporting male hand clasped hers, no chest swelled with pride beside her. But she had her baby.

My sister explained some simple procedures. The girl, for she was not much more than that, hardly listened for joy that a new life had come into this world. She shyly bared her breast and winced at the new sensation of that tiny mouth working so hard. Colostrum entered to protect the body from natural disease. During those same first moments, warm affection entered to protect the spirit from harm. There is love—our very life—our humanity.

In the favella of Rio, I have seen numberless cardboard hovels under bridges or on hillsides. Here too it happens. Elsewhere in

birthing rooms in pristine hospitals, so effi-
cient, so clean, it happens, as it did with my
wife. Whatever the circumstance, the Lord
God sustains those tender beginnings of
human response. The ability to love puts out
tender roots and begins to secure itself.

But these states need to be cultivated that
they may bear fruit. If we don't know how to
love and don't learn to trust, we will be
prejudiced. The security of being accepted, of
being at home, begins even in the very first
hours. Alienation, rejection, and insecurity
undermine our trusting of each other. The
first people we love in those first tender days
and months make a profound difference in
the fight against prejudice.

Usually no father is near in those South
African townships to see and hold the new
life, to proudly receive that precious package
from the midwife's hands. There is no supporting smile for the mother from her lover. In
earlier times he might have been away hunt-
ing to support his family, or tradition might
have dictated that birth was a purely female
thing. Still, in those times he was proud and
stood for something. There were meaningful
rites of passage. The family looked up to him
and understood if he were absent.

But change has relentlessly pressed in.
Social and religious values have eroded.
Perhaps on this special day the father is
working in distant mines, or perhaps less

fortunately, lounging, complaining and unemployed, in a hostel with many others like himself. Lonely and living away from home, he may escape to other women, to drugs, to drink. As an economic, social, or religious support for his family he is almost non-existent. When he returns, he often tries to cover for his neglect with assertiveness, frequently harshness. His guilty ambivalence often leads to another conception, and the cycle continues.

In the Chicago slum, despite all the initial kindled tenderness, there is a vacuum. No husband, no father, no man holds her hand or gently bends to kiss her. Perhaps the flow of her affection falters as she wonders who the father is. The infant needs her. She is tired. She must care for this treasure. But how? Is it a job for social service? How can a welfare check sustain these fragile bonds of love and security? Does she go back on the street with all its risks to both herself and the child? The cycle continues.

Thirty years ago in hospitals across our country, it was not only the facilities that were sterile. When some of my children were born, even the law ruled out my presence. Many fathers now go to birthing classes and are proud to be there. But too often it is a precious but temporary interlude, an important effort but an inadequate reform. Self-imposed or at least accepted as inevitable, the pressures

build. Demands on time, distractions press on
both the mother and the father. Studies of
quality time with the children multiply, but
the number of minutes spent with them grows
smaller and smaller.

Too often divorce occurs. I have no idea how
many cases I have seen. Sometimes it is just
abandonment, for no marriage existed. In a
hundred different ways, the challenge
becomes how to preserve the images of mother
and father without the roles of husband and
wife. Our affluent society sometimes meets the
financial needs, but too often, impersonally,
more and more mothers are left socially and
religiously alone. They turn to employment
outside the home not just for financial
security but to uphold their sense of being
someone. Where they looked for support and
appreciation they find instead unbearable
rejection by society in general and males in
particular. Their sense of inadequacy as
women and wives often makes them feel
inadequate as mothers as well. They turn to
work and day care.

I remember visiting a day care center where
my youngest daughter worked. The rows of
cribs with clean white sheets and kicking feet
stretched along the wall. There were cute animal pictures on the wall, a couple of rocking
chairs, and an area with safe toys where two
sweet babies crept and rolled. Diapers were
changed regularly. The head of the center

explained that though the providers vary, there is ample provision for "TLC". She led us to the next room on the tour and explained some of the guided "learning experiences" the little toddlers would pass through. "These ladies all have certificates; many have degrees in child care; of course they are all bonded." Imagine a new, uncertain and single Mom hearing about all this expertise. Will she feel intimidated, even inadequate? Will she try to focus on all the apparent benefits to convince herself that this type of care is right or at least necessary? With changing primary care givers, a different but significant cycle continues, profoundly affecting the ability of the child to love and to trust.

In the former townships I have watched the rhythmic sway of mothers walking, working, talking, and laughing, with infants slung on their backs. The intimacy of mother and child lasts longer here than in many cultures. Is there some mysterious psychological connection to the underlying warmth you sense among these people? Is it in infancy that they begin to learn to accept each other as brothers and sisters in a greater family? Later, when necessity occupies the mothers and the children need care, they turn to the grandmothers and older women. They are family too. Often it is the grandmothers who present the children for baptism.

In the American slum often it is a social worker to whom the mothers turn. Social workers grieve. Politicians argue. Responsibility for primary care may shift to trained hands, but hands often too over-loaded to provide a focused and caring "image". Once it begins its cancerous growth, it takes a lot to overcome a sense of abandonment and rejection by the natural mother. In the West, distance comes so soon—too soon. Where is the family haven of security, trust, and love, that first and deep-est antidote to prejudice?

What is happening to the Mother and Father images? In broadest human terms our Primary Care Giver is the Lord our God. It is He who made us, and He who provides for us. We are His children. He made male and female, that together they would learn to love each other and then to love their offspring until they come into their own right. In humanity's free and loving response to each other the harmony and wonder of creation can reach its height, if only we nurture and sustain it.

"God created man in His own image; in the image of God He created him; male and female He created them." As God is one, hus-band and wife should strive to become one, that their created difference may come together in the most basic relationship of human life. Their relationship is the role model for the child's beginning sense of human worth. As God cares for us, so we together should care for our children. Where are we? Where are we going? The same people who can only spare a few minutes of quality time for their children will often deplore prejudice. What are we thinking?

There is growing evidence that children think of their God in the same terms as they think of their primary care givers. In too many cases throughout the world the father, if present, turns his back, often appears unjust, and frequently harshly neglects the mother. The mother is often weak, caring but overcome with feelings of inadequacy. There is little sense of unity or depth of common purpose in the home, and yet we expect somehow to find it in society. Often neither father nor mother is a concerned and caring presence in the child's life. By our examples, the first idea of God as a Father we often give is that He is unjust, harsh, and neglectful or remote. If this is modified by the mother, God often appears caring, but weak and inadequate. The idea that He is a loving, all-wise, and caring presence Who draws people together is increasingly rare. One of the most important gifts we can give to our children is the knowledge that we love our spouses and that we are there.

Some of us try to answer prejudice simplistically by saying, "We are *all* children of one Heavenly Father." But we should think twice of what the words "Heavenly Father" might mean. If the Lord was the kind of parent we knew, or even the kind our own children know us to be, could He be the answer to prejudice? Conscience must not be founded upon sand or it can never stand up against prejudice.

Consider a possible alternative. My wife was in our own bed. The labor was hard, but I was there throughout. I never felt a stronger sense of tenderness. When the little blue hand turned pink, and the pink gradually spread to the fingertips, I wanted to sing and to cry. How dependent the new gift of life was! How dependent I am. As the new baby settled beside his mother, the miracle and wonder of it was overpowering. I kissed her forehead. A deep sense of peace and trust settled in the room. I wanted to pray. Later that night we did. In deep gratitude we joined hands and said together, "Our Father, who art in the heavens...."

During this time I had been privileged in another way. I had seen a woman so precious to me working hard, incredibly hard for life itself. From a covenant with her Creator, she labored with every fiber of her body in a mission which rose to an affectional level where I could only wonder, though I wanted so much to understand. How can a husband possibly watch his wife give birth without feeling profound awe before feminine courage and mystique?

Later I loved watching the bath; played with baby's feet, watching his toes curl. The first time I bathed him, the nurse who was teaching me said I held his arm so tight it cut off the circulation.

Many times as the days passed, the baby would stop sucking, but still hold on. My wife would look up and see me sitting across the room watching her. Something happened between us, precious and so assuring. Talking wasn't necessary. In the wonder of His creation that He shared with us, we were close to each other and to our God.

When my son was teething I held him sort of draped high over my shoulder. It may have seemed rough, but it worked miracles. My wife and I shared the night work. Often we were both awake and talked. We spoke of things we never seemed to think about during the day. Sometimes we were surprised at how much we agreed. Pleasantly, but still surprised. They were good times.

As the weeks went by, Ve planned the baby's schedule so that I could hold him until she could pat and smooth the corner of the table knowing that dinner was ready. After supper we let the dishes wait until the baby got a little fussy. We knelt in prayer beside his bed. One night he pulled himself up on the side of the bed and then dropped to a kneeling position. It was so innocent we stumbled over the familiar words.

Three months later when we finished the prayer, he said, "Amen." So clear. We both heard it. It was the first time.

When he first staggered between the dining room chairs, a new era of exploration began. He was confident, but on each new adventure he would look back over his shoulder as if to check that one or the other of us was there. We watched and wondered.

These last scenes have many elements that were not present in my first eighteen months of life, and they may not have been in yours. They are not reminiscences of the great way things used to be and never were. They simply sketch things which we did, trying to lay a foundation for the "Image" of a Heavenly Father Whom we hoped our son could love and trust. Anyone can focus on the budding needs for love and trust—and find their own way. Think. Reflect and do what you can. It will make a difference.

Fowler says, "The gift or emergent strength of this stage is the birth of imagination, the ability to unify and grasp the experience world in powerful images, and as presented in stories that register the child's intuitive understanding and feelings toward the ulti- mate conditions of existence. The dangers in this stage arise from possible possession of the child's imagination by unrestrained images of terror and destructiveness or from the witting or unwitting exploitation of her or his imagination in the reinforcement of taboos and moral or doctrinal expectations."[1]

Some of our most profound prejudices are born of terror and destructiveness in the imagination or, worse, in the reality of our first few years. There is much of witting and unwitting exploitation and taboos in the deeps of prejudice. If there is to be an answer, it will have its beginning in the ability to unify and grasp experience in powerful, loving human images. The beginning answers to prejudice are registered as intuitive understanding and feelings towards the ultimate conditions of existence. There is great power for humanity within these ultimate conditions.

But what about the mother in the township or the slum, or the struggling single parent? Maybe such scenes from my son's life are meant to inspire, but in reality do they discourage and depress? Do they cut the ground out particularly from under those who feel overpowered by circumstance? Perhaps.

---

1 Fowler, James W. Stages of Faith: The Psychology of Human Development and the Quest for Meaning. San Francisco: Harper & Rowe, 1981, p. 134

Think of creation again. None of the different trees controls the weather. Some are bent in the wind; some are stunted by drought; some are distorted by disease or infestation of insects. We too can be bent, stunted, and twisted. I was bent by being an "accident," particularly as this fact was blurted out in anger and frustration when I was quite young.

Unlike trees, we have an eternal soul, a plane of life which enables us to say of anything that comes our way, "You can do to me what you want, but you can't make me like it." The growth of our character is shaped not so much by circumstance as our response to it. Perhaps the beauty of our character is destined to be like that lonely twisted cypress on the California coast. But potential beauty is there for us to see and for others to appreciate.

The smallest gesture can carry great love, particularly when it overrides adverse circumstance. For example, later in life Ve and I learned a great deal from the deep sense of loss over multiple miscarriages. When you see the efforts, the sufferings, and the struggles of one you love, the closeness can be profound. Little things become big when love is in them.

Hard as the choice might be, the township husband could turn his back on drugs, drink, and other women. He could think of his wife and children rather than yield to his own urges to escape. Perhaps that's too much to expect. What if he brought home just a portion of the money he would otherwise spend? It would not change everything. They still might be hungry, but his wife and kids would know that he cared. There would be a change in the father image and a new opportunity for the Heavenly Father to assure the child that He cared too.

Or because he knows it is right in the Lord's eyes, the father could restrain his temper when he comes home. If his wife and children saw that effort, the father image would change. If their image of God became less angry, perhaps the children would be less angry. Perhaps they could pray more easily and even play more easily. A little thing could become big.

The new mother in the slum can nurse her baby as long as possible. She can be there for her baby. If society, if *we* care, we can open ways for her to be a mother, not to make us feel good about our gifts, to protect us from crime, or a thousand reasons demeaning of humanity, but because we believe in motherhood and the loving human trust it upholds. Our love can help her love. Even if betrayed in experience, she can learn that trust is not all a lie. We can perhaps become worthy of her trust. Perhaps she can be helped to discover others who, two or three, are gathered

together to try even in small ways to show
their babies that they love them.

In the simplest acts of love the Son of Man
can have a place to lay His head. Perhaps we
could form a league of surrogate grandmothers who could support those tiny potentials
from instinctive love. Somehow that mother
must be empowered to follow the instincts of
motherhood with dignity. She needs some
level of human acceptance in order to become
accepting. She needs to be able to count on
love, not just a program or a welfare check.
But sending money after a problem seems so
much easier than giving love.

You can travel the world and see the truth
in Maslow. In the hovels in Rio, the garbage
on the Chicago street, the dust and filth
blight the ability to trust and create an anger
which is the antipode to the love and concern
we so badly need. A belly distended by acute
hunger needs real food, not pie in the sky. In
a sense more profound than our affluent
society can ever sound, the concern for just
plain survival must be first in time. Physical
needs exert tremendous power to pull us
down from higher thoughts and motives.
They can create a victim mentality which is
excruciating in its impact on humanity.
These needs must be addressed.

Care for physical well-being is first in time,
but it must never be first in end. We who
strive to ameliorate the hunger for bread must

also learn to nurture with love, or we will fail. In poverty the need to survive is almost all-consuming. But the inner fight against poverty is not a battle for things, but rather through humanity to provide an opportunity for humanity. We spend so much effort fighting outward conditions and trying to change the world around us. But genuine human relationships are internal and real change is within us. Which means more, a husband bringing a few rand to his wife in the township, or a husband in a high-rise bringing home a dozen roses? We don't know, but the feelings of the husbands and the wives will tell. It is not the act itself but what it represents that is the real measure. The true measure of human worth is what we love, what we think about, and what we try to do. Our Lord will read our intentions, and our children, spouses, and true friends will look for what is behind our actions no matter how much we are hemmed in by circumstance.

The opportunities to change the circumstances in the world are limited. With the Lord's help the opportunity to change our hearts is unlimited.

11

---▼---

THE AWESOME WONDER OF IT
FACING THE MADE-UP AND REAL WORLDS

My Mom was a talented seamstress. Even in those early depression years she found work at my aunt's sewing studio next door. She specialized in baby clothes. I can still see the notched cut in the paper she used to measure the folds. My Dad said that she could hand stitch finer tucks in a baptismal gown than any he had ever seen. One of my deepest memories is how proud Dad was of Mom. He spoke of it openly and often.

Mom was a woman, completely different from Dad, but she was vitally important in his eyes. The very fact that she had qualities he did not made her a treasure to him. How lucky I was that my parents appreciated and honored their differences as husband and wife. A precious tool for understanding male and female differences was written as it were in invisible ink on my memory. Later, warmed by my own affectional needs, its clear message appeared. Sometimes I think that because it is so subtle, we misjudge the impact that the relationship between father and mother has on their children.

Children "see" much more than we realize. Watch them, the cloud of concern as they hear a harsh voice—the smile and giggle when they sense joy. Who knows when we first recognize the difference between the sexes? When we do, are we immediately aware of competition or of a complementary and loving relationship between our parents? The child learns long before he says their names that there is a difference between Mama and Daddy. The husband and wife relationship is more than an opportunity to learn to handle male and female difference. It is a cornerstone of learning to rise to the challenge of mutual needs in society. It is perhaps the first living example of how to handle human difference wherever we find it. Even the wide eyes of a little child can see and respond to tenderness and understanding between his two very different parents.

Certainly growing marriages are challenged. That is the way of growth. But what a

difference a stable marriage makes to the
children. They see love between two people
who care. The harmony, disharmony, or
absence of a rich and mutual mother-father
paradigm determines the nature of the family.
Even as the family is the greatest single influence on human development, so its handling
of differences between parents and between
siblings is the greatest single influence on
how we handle broader human differences
later. To overcome prejudice, we must face it
and work it through in the family itself. It is
much easier to make human differences a
great political or social cause than to patiently
and steadfastly resolve those differences in
our marriages and in our own homes.

I always knew Mom regretted having to
work outside of our home. We knew that she
wanted to be with us. That message of where
she would rather be meant the world to me as
a child of a working mother. It was not that
she was miles away. She worked next door.
But love is a sustaining presence, on call,
there when you need it. Not next door. Not a
phone call away. But right there. Too quickly
we learn to cover for its absence. I learned to
cover my longings and hold back my feelings.
I missed something even though I did not
know what. Covering our feelings is the
enemy of human closeness and a cordial host
for prejudice. How can you get to know and
respect other human beings if they or you

form the habit of covering appropriate and tender feelings?

Even little, well-intentioned things can reinforce a tendency to hold back. I have to mention one. Most of my aunts next door were heavy. Every time I went next door they insisted on giving me a big hug. I was rolled around and engulfed. Sixty years later I still cringe when I recollect the sensation. (Some say that hugging me today is like hugging a porcupine.) Despite the obstacles, I still love "the aunts," and for years after hugged them whenever I saw them. I suspect my bristles are far more attributable to my mother's absence than to my aunts' propensity to engulf. Fortunately I married thin and someone who was there for me and for our children, someone I could hug with impunity.

     *   *   *

Throughout its course, life is a blend of affection and thought manifested in even seemingly insignificant experience. To "belong" in his world, sustained by love, a child must discover an order in his experience that he can count on. You've seen it. A baby lies on the floor watching every move in "his" world. Dirty or clean, every object within reach goes into his mouth. He starts at loud noises, croons at sweet sounds. He may prefer nursing to the taste of new foods even if we carefully strain them ourselves. His life is ordered and he is secure and confident.

Then he walks; and runs, sometimes to you, sometimes from you. It's a new world; opportunities to discover and explore are everywhere. As he becomes aware of differences in sense experience, he gives those differences names. Just think of the implications of his saying "Mama" and "Daddy" and knowing the difference. Still, his ranging curiosity challenges the security and confidence that he brings with him from infancy. No longer can he just be laid on a blanket in a "safe" environment. When he goes for the electric cord he needs to learn "No." He has to learn the dangers of the hot stove. Too often hurt, and he pulls back in fear of the unknown or the different. But in the presence of those he has learned to love and trust he reaches out confidently and eagerly to new and different experiences. He is learning to face an exciting world with wonder and real courage. Prejudice can never be overcome without courage, including later the courage to face ourselves, our past, our present, and our future. The struggle against prejudice can never be won without self-control.

But it is not only objects that are safe and unsafe. People are safe and unsafe. The world the child knows centers on his experience of nature and of humanity. His world is egocentric. But the more others are a part of that world, the more it requires self-control. The child needs to learn not to hit the dog or lose his temper. But he can't hit his baby brother, either. Approved and disapproved behavior needs to be sorted out with real respect for the property and person of others. The long tension between control and self-control begins. And self-control is basic to all genuinely human relations. Without it the response to difference will be uncertain, unreliable and will feed doubts. Independence and interdependence are in the ring together, but it is the parental referee who makes sure we play by the rules, granting approval or disapproval, providing discipline.

The foundation of discipline is the love and trust carried forward from the previous states. It is clear that approval means the most when it comes from someone we love. Disapproval involves the possible loss of that treasured foundation of closeness. The most effective person to express approval or disapproval is the one who has the strongest affectional bonds to the child. My mother? Yes! My eleven year old babysitting sister? No! Sometimes in my sister's babysitting eyes everything I did was wrong. At other times when she got busy, I was left on my own and got hurt. We need the steadying hands of love in order to face the unknown with confidence. We need love when we go too far and are hurt.

Our uniqueness will be curtailed if we are overly protected or if we are overly neglected. If as children we are allowed to blossom, that blossoming will be rooted in the profound mutual love that was established through bonding. If that love is genuine, it will become a sustaining force for the birth of confidence in others and in our loving Heavenly Father. The immature trust in parental care prefigures our mature trust in Divine care. The gradual release which allows a child's independence to sparkle takes place not because we love our children less, but because we love them enough.

Prejudice will be conquered by the free and independent action of individuals, not by coercion, nor on the other hand by over-protecting the underdog. Being a good father is never paternalism, but it is being there. We don't often hear of maternalism. Being a good mother involves steady and ready-to-hand nurturing, but never maternalism. Some of the supposed solutions to prejudice are frankly paternalistic or maternalistic—and they stunt human growth.

It is useful to reflect that conscience involves learning what our Heavenly Father approves and what He disapproves. It is not just learning to obey His commands from fear. It is learning to do what will please Him, because from love we want to.

Within loving parental care and protection, our Heavenly Father is preparing the way for that time when we can explore human difference and without fear learn to understand it and appreciate it so that we can work together for the common good. If we let it, human variety can perfect natural society even as it subsequently perfects heaven.

Will it be anger and fear or self-control and courage? My oldest son had such a temper that he had to be physically restrained lest he hurt himself. I remember holding his thrashing body down on the bed behind me, with my back turned so that in his childish way he did not feel he was getting the attention he was seeking.

The toddler soon discovers frustration in his world and frequently responds with temper. Anger is unpredictable and destructive. If parents respond with anger, it spawns fear and uncertainty in a child. Such fears can be repressed. It takes concerned care to avoid repression and work through our frustrated and angry moments. Prejudice feeds upon anger. It cries out to be worked through.

Our oldest also refused to go to bed because he was plagued with imaginary fears. We tried explaining them away, but the more we explained the more he felt that we were accepting the "nail animals," and the more real they became. Finally in desperation, following a book on child psychology, we pinned

him like a cocoon in a sheet and left him to
face "them." In less than half an hour he
asked to be released and never complained
again. Many could debate if his fear was cru-
elly repressed or courageously worked
through. What I think was accomplished: he
knew we who loved him would do our best to
help him through his anger and face his fears.
Many of us prefer to avoid even meeting differences, rather than to courageously face the
"nail animals" of prejudice.

Anger and fear are best met at inception
with measured firmness and love. Repressed
fears can lead to future conditioned and
uncontrolled feelings and acts of prejudice.
But psychology has demonstrated that even
future mindless and prejudicial reactions,
like fears, can be understood and worked
through. If we have lived them we must take
responsibility for them. Recognizing their
impact on our reaction to others is the first
step. But changing our way of life and seeking
forgiveness must follow. Just as a child finds
parental forgiveness at the end of his short
dark tunnels, we will find Divine forgiveness
at the end of our long ones. But without a
clear recognition of right and wrong, forgiveness is meaningless. If there is no wrong,
what's to forgive? To be judgmental is to base
judgment on false or prejudicial standards.
Very necessary righteous judgment is based
on truth—but sustained by love. It should

come as no surprise that self-control involves facing some frustration. But we can never work out our differences without covenants, rules held in common, and the self-control to live by them.

It is then irresponsible cruelty to put children out to graze before they know the difference between what is right and wrong. If we turn them out without boundaries they will inevitably find an uncertain world, unforgiving and unloving.

I remember the mud brick huts with their sheet metal roofs sown randomly throughout a small hot West African village. Children, chickens, and goats run freely on the hard packed trails and "streets" between the houses. There is something precious as the mothers un-self-consciously and without self-righteousness nurse their babies or carry them in slings of cloth on their backs. They are close, the babies and their mothers. The littlest toddlers venture around the dirt floor or at least within range of the mothers' babbling. Perhaps it is words, but I do not understand Twi. Like the glorious harmony of their voices, old and young in song, even the little toddlers are tuned to community.

Love is there. Effective disapproval and approval are there. Fear or acceptance are right there. The toys are a bit of cloth, a stick, or an odd-shaped stone, transformed and made living and wonderful by the imagination. The games are simple and happy. In every direction there is a world to explore with confidence. "It takes a village," not a sociologically conjured and government sponsored substitute, but the greater family of a village founded upon the love of parent and child.

On the other side of the world I've been in homes where the little person sits in the midst of bright plush and plastic, and hugs his dirty old blankie. The multiplication of things is no answer. Look behind the things at the depth and breadth of the response. One of the wonders of development is the way curiosity drives it from the familiar to the new and exciting. Then it looks for ways to assimilate the experience, to explain it, to make it familiar and accept it. The family often repeats my childhood reaction to Christmas shopping: "Too many legs and feet." Too many activities, too many toys, too much going on, does not allow the mind to assimilate and interpret. Humanity is not measured by the accumulation of things, but by putting them in their place. In human terms most of us have quantities of bright plush and plastic friends, but have few dirty-old-blanket friends.

I remember one trip to a village above the escarpment in Ghana. The car bounced towards the market. Inside I was the one white among five blacks. We had stopped to let the driver siphon and spit gas into a hot and dry carburetor. I was tired. We all were. From nowhere a child, then six, then twelve, ran beside the car shouting, "Brunie, brunie." My companions explained that "brunie" means "white man." I was the first white man most of them had seen. They have not known racial contrasts, but can we say they were unprejudiced? As I settled in my room their faces crowded the door, and I thought of the animal at the zoo when school kids crowd in awe and curiosity in front of its cage. I sensed that their new experience would lead to prejudice or not depending in large measure on me. I was a minority example and felt awkward. Picture it! Think of the opportunity! The responsibility! But particularly think of the ingredients on both sides. Circumstances brought us together in a way which was new to all of us, but our deeper affections and how they were read determined the still hidden outcome.

My family loved to tell the story of my sister and mother boarding a train to go East to see my grandparents. I've heard similar experiences described by a number of friends. The black porter blossomed at the joy of having a child in his Pullman car. Moments later he rumbled with laughter. His eyes sparkling, he confided to my mother, "She wants to know why I don't wash my dirty face and hands." He was the first black person my sister had seen. Think of the ingredients! I too went many years without any significant experience with blacks. Did that make me more or less prejudiced? Assimilating and accepting human difference will not come from simply experiencing it.

No matter when it occurs, naive experience of racial difference will be interpreted. The question is how? Simply being exposed to human difference as in the former townships or the inner city is not the answer. Particularly it is no answer without the steadying hands of loving adults to guide and foster the experience. Human acceptance must involve confident emotional balance and a system of approved and disapproved values between people, or the acceptance and/or rejection will be literally skin deep.

In many homes in this country, black mothers, on the basis of their own experience, try to prepare their children for the hurt of discovering unequal treatment as they enter a diverse and, unfortunately, too often unaccepting world. It may be preparing them for reality, but it also teaches them to expect prejudice and, within that expectation, it may even breed hidden shame. What if by happy circumstance the hand of acceptance and friendship were extended? Will they be open and receptive or hesitant and suspicious? Such values begin early, and with extreme subtlety. Will it be shame, doubt, and guilt or initiative and autonomy?

I have watched children of different races playing happily together. The exposure to difference is there. One mother stands by and patronizingly says to her friend, "It's so cute to see them playing together." She totes up her supposed lack of prejudice like a golf score. Another parent says nothing, but feels an inexplicable cold; what if? Her whole body tenses as she sees a little black boy give a big hug to her white daughter. The children are tuned to sense experience and read the eyes, the movements, the tone of voice of the adults. The boy could not put them into words, but he adroitly reads the reactions. He won't hug her again. Interpretation is subtle, so subtle, so early.

For kids today the opportunities to experience differences have multiplied. Sometimes, as in day care centers and schools, it happens by law. Sometimes it happens by conscious and conscientious moral design. On the other hand, sometimes black and white are put together because it is the "in" thing. The reasons why blacks and whites get together as kids are varied. But they are getting together. It's happening. And often it's happening before racial prejudice has taken root. The richer and the more positive the experience in childhood, the more powerful the potential counterbalance to prejudice will be in later life. But the basic humanizing tools of love, trust, right and wrong, and still later a conventional covenant of respect for others must also be there. The opportunity for tolerance may be born of experience, but acceptance itself reaches to our very being and is a free gift of the growing spirit.

Today I watch black children and white children happily playing together, and I wish their attitudes could always be so. But on my part I realize that I am not just watching kids having fun together. I'm still watching black kids play with white. Sometimes I want to stop an argument a little more quickly. The hard fact is, I still notice. I am still color conscious. The kids will always be different individuals. I will always see differences. But the problem is that when I see black and white kids, it isn't the same as seeing blondes and brunettes. Should it be? Are cultural and racial differences deeper than the difference between blond and brunette? Do I try too hard? Change can only come through trying. But prejudice is an attitude: how and why we act and react the way we do. Still, these are new generations. They will not all be like me. Thank goodness!

I can imagine two little toddlers, one black, one white, running back and forth between suburban yards. Their mothers are laughing and talking about how to conquer the thistles which are blowing over from an as yet undeveloped part of the subdivision. Later the kids sit side-by-side on the same school bus. There will be matter-of-fact acceptance. The parents and the children are largely color blind. Experience has provided the opportunity; and that same experience has been interpreted from day one by deeply held convictions of conscience. Perhaps it is a premature dream. Perhaps it is generations off. But that day can, indeed must come. If the heart is there, time will make a difference. If the heart is not there, calling for time is merely an excuse.

But prejudice is moderated by how we experience the world as well as how we experience its inhabitants. Our babies loved to be put out under the trees where they could look up and watch the trembling leaves. I remember the gurgles of laughter as I dangled our babies' feet in a bubbling stream. They seemed to be kindred spirits, bubbling, gurgling, and laughing at each other.

I have watched toddlers run to and fro in stumbling response to the waves slipping up and down a sandy shore. On the lawn their chubby bare feet pulled back at the prickles of the short spring grasses. Wonder built upon wonder. They accepted newness. They were not afraid, because strong hands were near.

They sucked in their breath. They wondered, and they questioned. That's the key: they questioned. Experience demands interpretation. The rich panorama can inspire a sense of confidence and trust in our Maker, or it can be but a momentary blip on the too busy screen of life. Both belonging in the world and belonging among the people of the world shape our person. Every sensation, every experience, stirs up an affection. Drawn together in patterns, they begin to form a sense of wonder and order or of fear and disorder.

The other day my three-year-old grandson was visiting. I went to the garden and picked the first cherry and regular tomatoes, brought them into the kitchen, and unconsciously arranged them in order of size on the counter. Moments later my daughter came in and said to my grandson, "Oh, look! See the tiny tomatoes and look how they get bigger and bigger. Which do you want in your salad?" The lesson of size difference was not fitting plastic cups together, but instead was real and directly related to his life.

Eating, whether tomatoes or poi, is something we all do. Eating together as families is more rare than it used to be. My kids used to report how their friends asked in disbelief, "You mean you eat breakfast together?" Our kids' school had no school lunch program. I also worked nearby. My wife used to almost resent my coming home for lunch because lunch was so much a time dedicated to sharing with the kids. If I was there, she felt her attention was divided. Is there some way we can be as concerned for our mental diet as our physical?

I remember my wife's taking our little preschoolers down to the brook behind our house. There, among the mushrooms and mosses they built fairy lands—soft warm and happy places amid the cheering voices of the birds and the soothing ripples. Somehow, for a time, living happily ever after was real to them. Is there not a carry-over to the mature hopes we dare to bring to reality in later life? Do not those who have promised their love try day by day to infill with reality the promise of "ever after?"

Princes and Princesses rule kingdoms of justice and fairness. In the fairy lands of life good conquers evil, and happiness and love are forever. I believe such strong feelings reinforced day by day are a vital foundation from childhood for finding our way to a better society. They form a bridge from the warmth of home and family to an idealized society. Our society's cynical distrust of almost every profession is a highly contagious disease to pass on to our children. We need a potential idealized alternative to the real world which presses in on us soon enough. We need it lest we later forget to raise the questions, "Is all this necessary? Is it right?"

Mentors can guide the experience and often lead the affections. They can provide a sense of wonder and of meaning, the wonder of variety. Experience can be merely random, or all part of an emerging Divine scheme. We can pragmatically manipulate it, or you and I can responsibly live and move in it. A sense of wonder before the variety of creation can inspire a sense of wonder before human diversity. Being created by God, every one of us is potentially in the image and likeness of our Maker. What wonder is here! What human potential! As He is our Father, so is He our Creator. What a wonderful word "our" is! So different from, yet inclusive of "mine" and "yours."

The child not only walks, he talks,—and later talks, and talks. We had tropical fish as our first family "pets." My oldest son used to spend hours watching them flash back and forth under the light. His first word was not "Daddy" or 'Mama" but 'fish.' I remember because it hurt my feelings. Still, a goldfish or plant in a tenement, a tree growing in Brooklyn can testify to the Essential. The Wonderful is in the simplest things, if we have the eyes to see Him. Compare a complex of experience which mystifies to a simple experience which, when assimilated, testifies. Is it to be a dozen plastic trucks or one Teddy bear or even one stick doll in Africa? Is television discovery too often violent and scary? Even if "interactive," does it feed human warmth one to another?

As the toddler explores, he pieces together his various sensations and learns to identify objects. He associates that identification with specific sounds, and language is born. Think of it! The whole of language is based upon the perception of distinctions and differences. His budding imagination enables him to group sensations into distinguishable objects which he can name. It is his way of beginning to make sense of them. He sees the unique qualities which separate them from others. The "who" and "what" of life come first. The "doing" words and the "why" words rapidly follow, identifying and defining human response. Nouns, verbs, adverbs, and adjectives spring to life in order. Soon language becomes a means of expressing simple thoughts and affections. The babysitter comes and tries to put her charge to bed. He says, "I uh blanie." The sitter doesn't understand. His frustration blurts, "Blanie, blanie, blanie!" Still no understanding. Then tears. Prejudice against sitters is reinforced.

*   *   *

Relating to other people involves communication of content and sphere. Books were rare in our home, but my father was a tremendous story-teller. He spun tales of "Hiram and Mirandy's" settling the West with all the details he had gleaned from working as a kid in the Colorado mines. Later he told, with some embellishment, his experiences in France during the First World War. I can still picture his shooting down a German plane with a pan machine gun. Even though he was a medic, he got mad when the plane strafed the hospital tent. I remember sitting on the couch beside him or on the floor at his feet, depending on who won the race to get there first. It was our quality time.

My wife's mother read to her almost every day. So did her nanny. She felt a special closeness to both as they shared the wonders of Tasha Tudor, the Petershams, Kate Seredy, Dorothy Lathrop, and dozens of others whose work was so familiar she could recite the stories by heart. The imagery and the stories built a mythical happy land of promise—but it throbbed with affection as she cuddled next to her mother.

Those times when our kids cuddled close to their mother to hear a story were precious for the content *and* the accompanying chords of humanity and closeness. When I read or sang, their heads pressed against my arm to see the pictures, I could almost physically feel the tender sharing of the spirit.

My oldest son is a talented amateur actor. He goes to child-care centers to tell stories to little ones. He has skills to feed the imagination beyond those of most parents. The kids get something very important, but parents' reading, even if wooden and stumbling, adds an irreplaceable ingredient. Some of our primary schools have class Grandmas who come and read. Single parents might uncover a precious communication tool if we showed them the way to get the books and found ways to give them the time to read to a little package snuggled close.

It is hard to realize that affections and thoughts are more real than bread and milk. We try to pick up on the lingo of a child who is learning our own language by tuning into their gestures and expressions. Yet it is often words and deeds which seem to divide us from different nationalities. When we literally are calling the same object a different name, it is an open invitation to misunderstanding. The *wrong* way and the *long* way sound the same to a Japanese person. Even in the same language, Etonian and Cockney signal different classes. There's a lot of difference between a Southern accent and that of Brooklyn, and the difference often carries a measure of prejudice with it. How many remember the English language goulash of boot camp? Honestly, when you call an 800 number and an unfamiliar accent answers, do you sigh inside? Honestly? Instead, you could smile and try to picture the person behind the accent and guess their origins.

Languages have different grammars and word orders too. These in turn subtly influence the patterns of thought, and can fuzzy the communication. Mutual understanding and communication are key to accepting other cultures. Simple exposure to different languages may be useful but in itself is not the answer. There may be a thousand different words for the tree outside of my window, but the idea of that tree in our various minds is almost the same. Focus on the words and we are divided; focus on the thoughts and affections and we come together.

A tree or even a stone can inspire a plethora of different affections as well as thoughts. I remember in Greece plaiting a few branches of a bush into a wreath as I watched a little boy running around an ancient track in Olympia. We shared no words, but when I placed the wreath on his head, we shared much more. Gradually these affections reach to the depths of our consciousness. How glorious it is when we learn to share this inner poetry of life! These are the levels that must open or reopen in order to discover our potential relation to others, our humanity. The wonder of it! uncovering our different paths to those deeply held loves we have in common. In Fowler's terms, it is a mythical and lyrical faith. It anchors our being with promise like the promise of a new sprouting sapling.

Many whites as well as blacks and orientals are fascinated with trying to trace their roots. Perhaps they are seeking a basis for pride or dreams. It is hard to know what motivates an avid genealogist. It seems like a great place to start, but a precarious place to stop, for knowledge of cultural origins can cut both ways, either nurturing or mitigating prejudice. Roots are not the only thing that determine the nature of the tree. Many, perhaps most of us at times, try to probe the mystery of those powerful affections from childhood which bend or even twist our natures. The wind, storm, and sunshine moments of our early years powerfully shape the life we become. Some are imbedded in our nature and like the trunk of a tree cannot be changed. But pruning and shaping, even feeding the soil, are all options, which like conscious reflection and response can revisit and rework our responses to life. As responsible adults we can look to the shape and usefulness of our own lives in the context of the variety which confronts us. But never forget the opportunity for change among the saplings which God has committed to our care.

Look at a little child as he slowly moves a toy back and forth, or looks up from a book. His eyes say he is in another world. Who can tell what images are going through his mind? Are they racing? Or is his imagination simply drifting on some peaceful flow? Many of us must re-learn how to feel deeply.

We turn on the TV or the radio to jam our outer thoughts so we don't have to look within. Too many are afraid of silence and solitude. But if you cannot face yourself, can you really face others? Reflecting on early childhood, our own and as we observe it, can uncover some of the purest springs of our humanity. Those wells need to be dug again, if we would overcome prejudice.

III

▼

Wow! School

Beyond Family: School, Peers and Conventional Rules

Wow! School! The excitement. Even Mom was keyed up. I knew all the kindergartners. Miss Jenny, my teacher, lived ten houses away. My stomach tightened. The smell and skid of new Crayolas, the clash and bang of rhythm band, fighting for the big drum, more and bigger blocks than I had ever seen. Everything went great until skipping. Movement was vital to Miss Jenny, and I had to come back to afternoon school to learn to skip. I was different. Everyone else, the whole world knew how to skip.

Later, the first grade teacher tried to keep all of us after school for talking. I was different again. I had done nothing wrong, so I decided to go home. I can still feel the soft sponginess of her as I punched my way through her and out the door. I was sure that Mom would back me up. She backed me up all right, right upstairs to write an apology, and no food until it was accepted.

Mom was on the phone immediately to the teacher, apologizing—Mom apologizing for me! What I had done was not just uncomfortable for the teacher or anyone else; it hurt Mom; it was wrong. I did not have the right to be different at the expense of love and respect for Mom, or any adult.

Mom was adamant about order as one key to fairness. If you had no respect for others, you had very little in her eyes. She'd just start humming her mad song ("Santa Lucia"), and you knew something was coming. We, not society, were the cause of good or bad behavior. We were the ones who would make something of ourselves or not. "Who do you think you are?" I guess my first grade teacher just didn't know "Santa Lucia."

Actually, we had three grades in one classroom. Coping with older bullies and girls four or five inches taller was a heavy burden at times. One of the girls could hit a ball farther than any of us. But we learned to aspire after both the good and the bad that we didn't have yet. Our world was more diverse than some, and in it we learned to work independently or fail. And with Mom, failure was not an option.

An enormous mound of mud and clay lumps stood where they were building a new house. One of the boys, a class ahead, was on top of the mound chucking big lumps at the girls. Though the girls were giggling and dodging, not running away, I started up the hill to stop his injustice. As soon as my face got even with his fist he knocked me sprawling down the hill. Chivalry was not dead, but it had very little dignity left.

In a sense, primary school students live in two worlds—an idealized dream world and a down-to-earth world where they learn self-control and discipline. Our sense of justice gives meaning to order. We wrestle with ourselves to become something special among our friends.

We develop a religious ideal founded on love and trust and a sense of belonging—a sort of continuation of the fairy tale view of life. In that paradigm justice always wins. When I was innocent and was still kept after school, that view was hurt. It was tough sitting in the dirt at the bottom of the hill. It wasn't fair for a girl who should be a princess to hit a baseball so much farther. My idealized faith struggled to find consistency between my Mom's domain and school's, between prince and just plain boy. Good has to be approved and rewarded in our idealized worlds, and evil has to be punished. But under the stress when it doesn't happen, we begin a lifelong process of sorting for ourselves. Is it our fault? Can we lay it on others? These are the same questions races ask themselves when they are under the stress of injustice. The same questions rejected spouses ask when marriage fails. Is it me?

As we move into school and group activities, a tension develops between our ideal world where we can be heroes and the practical world of learning, playing, and getting along with others who want to be heroes too. We learn the rules. We begin cheering for our team. We want to cooperate in order to win. The luxury of being a loner passes. We enter a kind of tyranny of the "they."

Since the teacher is at first a surrogate parent, the more harmonious the parent-teacher value system, the less deeply traumatic our transition to school. Private or parochial schools that uphold this harmony can nurture and infill the mythical religious ideal as an underlying motivation for the future development of faith. These ideals become a kingdom of justice, of God within. In ideal circumstances good peer leaders and heroic role models in real life are in tune with these same values and help us give them day-to-day underpinnings.

Our dream world becomes a world of more and more realistic hope.

I went to a parochial school. Of course we had religion classes. We were also told that we learned to read so we could read the Word of God for ourselves. We learned arithmetic because it was a way of working with and defining God's order. Science was a study of God's creation. We learned history because it testified to God's Providence. We learned to write so that we could communicate charitably with our neighbors. All these things, even at that age, made us think more deeply about life. But as time passed, our functional values in daily decisions were confirmed by the reactions of our friends. Genuine values of the kind that can stand up to prejudice are both left and right brained, taught and acquired by example, intellectual and affectional.

As we moved on to grades 4, 5 and 6, I learned who the Chicago Cubs were. I got to go to the occasional Saturday matinee Western. The local merchants even provided outdoor free movies on a canvas screen wavering in the breeze one night a week during the summer. Whether the scandal mongers weren't as virulent, or whether less scandal existed, Bing, Abbott and Costello, and the Duke were pretty heroic, each in his own way. Psychologists say, "Let them want to be prima ballerinas or big league players. Let them try it and so discover their limitations for themselves. Maturity will put childhood's idols in proper perspective." While childhood's idols are gradually re-examined and reduced to normalcy, childhood's successful heroes still play a part in defining our human potential. The fact that someone has done it provides a beginning point of reality for the dramatic and romantic dream worlds of our imagination.

When my oldest son began public school, the suburban Denver community we lived in faced expanding migration from the inner city. The principal of the school tried every method to handle the diversity she met in the halls and classrooms every day. One day, much to their distress, she even called in a bunch of parents, handed them belts, and told them to spank their kids. She was trying to uphold a common rule of law.

My oldest son's mythical faith was particularly challenged by such diversity as he encountered such things as swearing, fights, dirty talk, and the rest in one life situation after another. He was still drawing pictures of knights and ladies. Those who cherish the "real" world and preparation for it would no doubt say it was high time that he worked it through. I say, "No." Strong reinforced ideals provide for vision throughout life. The transition from early childhood's myths and ideals into the more controlled-day-to day environment of peer group social behavior should be gradual, not traumatic. Life can and will be de-mythologized soon enough. We need a rich altruistic vision of life which lifts the spirit to hope, yes, for things unseen and undemonstrable.

In a South African urban black community, a young black boy sees a white boy his age riding in a new car eating ice cream. He turns to his Grandma and asks, "Why?" She knows all the implications of "Why" inscribed in his eyes and face. She recalls the days when young boys his age proudly led the flocks off to tend them during the day. She remembers her father returning from the hunt—proud to be providing. She knows the myths of the greatness of the Zulus; she has heard them since childhood. Are they a real answer to his "Why?" to those hungering and hurt eyes? Is the comparatively new Christianity, one of the white man's gifts, the answer? Isn't one of its teachings, "Ye shall know them by their fruits?" She answers with sadness and uncertainty. With childlike keenness, he reads her doubt and hesitation. A cultural ideal, the source of mythical faith, is dying and it's dying too young. Is there, will there be a sure replacement? There must be.

I caught something of the animistic spirit in the Midwestern corn fields. Our parents and teachers made a real effort to connect the intricate marvel of creation with every robin, squirrel, or spider we saw. I am deeply grateful for the love of nature they shared. It is not the basis of my belief, but it has become a daily living testimony illustrating and confirming my faith.

Think of the wonder of the umbrella of the jungle and the awesome daily miracles it shields. The tangle is full of hidden dangers, particularly to the uninitiated. But the glory of God is there too, for those tuned to His creation. There is a powerful sense of eternity and belonging in primitive religion. The native American felt it too under the majesty of the virgin forests or before the expanse of the boundless prairie. But for many the time when nature is alive in their hearts is cut short. Even as the chain saw snarls and tears at the shadows of the forest, a supposed realism cuts at the mystery of sprites, fairies, and gnomes. Childhood's symbols of the wonder of creation and Creator are, as it were, sacrificed to the veneer of a cocktail table. The carvings which testified to a world alive with meaning are now cottage crafts to gain a few dollars from the tourist whenever he comes out from behind his video camera.

So the denuded forests proclaim the failure of two cultures to successfully come together in God's name. If we accepted, understood, and fed childhood's Elysian world, how much better we would understand the emerging nations. The curriculum of creation is so rich, if only wonder and analysis learn to view it together.

There were no Blacks, Orientals, or Latinos in my school. It was not by design; there just weren't any in the whole town's population of nineteen hundred individuals. There were Republicans and Democrats, and I was a very lonely sunflower for Landon during Roosevelt's rise. Politics was very prominent in those depression days, and we kids joined in.

We hear the tension expressed between idealism and reality as we call for political leaders with vision and principle. We hear it in the increasing choice of schooling at home rather than in the public system. We hear it from what some scathingly call "the religious right," but who themselves would be horrified to be called the "irreligious left." All my growing years, in fact most of my life, I have held ideals which were not accepted by the Presidents or Congress. How much more disillusioned must be the South African black whose ideals have been confronted by apartheid all his life. Who are his heroes? Who are the heroes of those who roam the streets of our own inner cities? Where is their field of dreams; how rich is it, and how long does it last?

On my last trip to South Africa I sensed a change among my black friends. They feel deep concern about civil unrest and disorder. And they have reason for great concern. I've seen holes from stray bullets in the door of the garage of one of my black friends. The son of another was shot dead while walking his friends home after choir one Friday night. His murderer hoped to gain a few rand. Friday is pay day, and he was well dressed. My own daughter's family living in Durban was held at knifepoint, little innocent kids, while their home was robbed by a young black whom they had earlier tried to help.

The gangs still drape themselves on the dusty corners. Let a rival gang approach, and they are roused and energized as hidden weapons come out. It is sad because it seems so fruitless. But there is also a new sense of hope, a struggling to find and take responsibility which at long last the civil law has granted them. I pray that the leadership, no matter what bitterness history has spawned, will have the wisdom to protect the civil rights of the white minority. I pray too that the people will possess their souls with patience, keeping the engine of change running, but not allowing it to run away with them into chaos.

Civil order is only a means, but it is a necessary basis for moral and spiritual justice. Nations, like people, go through stages of growth. South Africa has great potential. It could become the economic engine to drive the development of Africa. But more than that, its people have an opportunity to redis-

cover a mythic ideal, to form just and fair
conventional rules, to build opportunities for
a new-found ability to choose and rise not
just economically but morally and spiritually.
It will not be easy, for through no fault of
their own true heroes are scarce and childhood's dreams have too often gone hungry.
And sadly, they must accommodate to a
Western culture which is all too short of
dreams as well.

By way of an as yet incomplete illustration:
In this country, civil rights legislation has
been a major step in controlling words and
deeds in society and in the work place. It is an
achievement to which Martin Luther King
could point with pride if he were here. But I
suspect that he would be the first to point out
that he had much more in mind when he
spoke the famous words, "I have a dream."
His dream tried to inspire in both blacks and
whites a moral sense of respect and fairness.
But the context of the speech and its subse-
quent influence makes clear that he asked for
a change in God's name. He called out for us
to be human with each other because it is
God's will that we should. He advocated an
ideal, a dream, appealing to that underlying
sense of justice and fairness which childhood
fosters. He also called for civil law as a basis
to allow that dream to mature and go forward.
But the vision he inspired must not stop with
civil reform. It must rise to mutual respect,

freely given, simply because we want to be
brothers under our God.

Nelson Mandela faces a similar challenge.
Both Martin Luther King and Mandela have
been criticized for their liberal associations
and even alleged communist ties. Emerging
nations and peoples tend to turn to those
whom they believe care and will help with the
immediate problems they face. They look for
peers, not colonialism-tainted and oppor-
tunistic paternalism. Their convictions may
have been quite different from what their
actions seemed to our eyes. They saw apparent economic benefits. South Africa was miles
from Russia, and there seemed to be little
direct or immediate threat to their freedoms.

I saw something of this particularly
through the friendship of my oldest son with
a South African black whom I had helped
bring to our College at the height of
apartheid. The young South African
espoused communism and openly criticized
our country's policies. Many of my conservative friends were scandalized and still bristle
at the very mention of his name. My son and
he came from such different backgrounds.
Yet they were both struggling at the age when
having a heart is far more important than
having a head. I simply could not keep my
mouth shut all the time, but I spent a lot of
time listening as each of them tried to sort
out for his own country a system of govern-

ment that he could identify with fairness and justice. I smiled wisely and wondered what the real answer was.

Today that same South African, after a self-imposed exile here, is working for the New South Africa. Many emerging nations opportunistically espoused communism, but never married it. I think it was probably true of my son's friend, despite his argumentative exterior. We all loved his father. In a conversation in our home the father tried so hard to restrain the son he regarded as a rebel while his son talked back to one he loved but regarded as an Uncle Tom. Both, but particularly the father, were embarrassed at being carried away in front of a white. It is so hard to really identify with the pressures others feel—but at least we can take a big step if we acknowledge that the feelings exist.

Mandela has turned on the powerful force of an idealized world where justice prevails. No one knows if he or his successors can bring forward fair economics and political law to support a just, conventional socicty. Like an elementary student, the country is trying to bring reality to its idealized world. But, as in education, the real answers involve growth far beyond this vital early step.

The wrenchings and blasts of prior disorder and injustice have almost stripped the tree of reason. Violence like lightning has struck and torn even the trunk. But deep within a voice says, "There is such a thing as a resurrection tree."

In many ways our country too is still in early elementary school in regard to race relations. Some, never having learned the lessons of infancy and applied them to race, still do not trust and are frankly scared. But many more idealistically hold to a sense of inner justice without seeing or facing the cruel reality. They climb the mud hill until they get punched. They see enough to accept most of the dictates of civil law and are outraged at the disorder of others. But when injustice touches them they want to punch their way out. Some see other races and cultures as if they are girls five inches taller who can always hit home runs.

Many call for reason. But reason demands the ability to sort out the important from the unimportant. It involves preventing the emotions from running away with judgment. Our founders were rationalists and were compelled by reason to acknowledge God-given human rights. There are times when I think they were more mature in their faith than most are today.

Part of reason's challenge is to sort out the important from the trivial, particularly in human relationships. Proper early education brings with it the precious gift of obedience and self-control. Without the ability to control ourselves under the same rules as our neighbor's we think and act emotionally, not rationally. If civil law falters in upholding order, rational human relations will stumble as well.

In the townships during the later years of apartheid, truancy was rampant. Kids were thrown into classes taught in a language they did not understand. If they came at all they came from backgrounds of grazing in gangs on the dusty streets. Hot and over-crowded classrooms. Inadequate supplies. Poorly trained teachers. One of my black friends in South Africa, sensing the chaotic danger in the breakdown of education, is running a private remedial preschool. His goal is to do more than teach preparatory English. In his school there is order and self-control and parental cooperation and support. One hopes the foundation for rea-son is being laid firmly enough to stand the tremors of social change, no matter what they measure on the Richter scale.

Society itself cannot exist without the orderly imposition of civil law to provide a foundation for the exercise of genuine human rights. Think of the need for order to provide for group understanding and acceptance in the elementary school classroom. It is not just formal religious instruction that is now lack-ing in public schools. Often just plain order is challenged. Now think of the place of civil law and order in providing for understanding and acceptance in society. Do we expect to solve our differences with childhood's tools for controlling behavior? Simple extrapolations of fear of punishment and unrealistic ideals and goals are not the way for a mature nation. All useful relationships require order. But order is never enough at the expense of heroic ideals. Mandela and his vision are South Africa's rainbow after the storm. Can human trust be restored? Can he continue to sustain a faith which aspires to God-given respect for all individuals? Can the conventions of civil law be established in time and be upheld by choice?

Human difference also often comes out in economic terms. The basis of prejudice can be simply a matter of "haves" and "have nots." I'm not referring simply to having or not having money. Some girls have looks, others don't. Some boys have macho bodies, others wimpy ones and, like the poor fellow in the ads of old, get sand kicked in their faces. Sex appeal varies. You name it, there are haves and have nots. But still the amount of money people have creates an easily perceived difference and is therefore a source or at least a support of prejudice. It is unquestionably a factor in most emerging nations.

One of my less proud elementary school memories: One day my friends and I pressed one of the neighbor's kids. "What did you have for breakfast?" "Mush." "What did you have for lunch?" "Mush." "What do you think you'll have for supper, Mush?" And we laughed and laughed. In those depression years, our family didn't have much, but we had more than mush. Mom would have killed us if she knew what we had done. Making fun of others was a definite, "No." And "No" meant "No" at our house. We were "haves" in relation to some of the neighbors. But we were "have nots" in many other ways. The real driving motivation was not circumstance, but our desire to define ourselves as we began to live with peers.

Economic prejudice is stiff and brittle, but it often masks deeper prejudices. It's hard to buy your way out of economic prejudice. When blacks drive their long shiny Cadillacs, for example, the symbol of having made it often masks the deeper prejudice as a white looks down on them from his Ford. Of course no one should be denied the opportunity of acquiring such things. But putting on fancy clothes or eating in the best restaurants won't gain us respect. It's the surface, not the cause.

When I first went to Rio as a church administrator I was struck by the contrasts. With some of the wealthy church members, I had formal multi-course meals: fish course, meat course, two or three wines, the whole served in a lush apartment in Copacabana. But I also remember visiting another home, a tiny house curtained off into two rooms. Half a dozen round-eyed kids watched and waited to see if I would take the proffered second piece of cake before they got theirs. At that time in Rio there was real economic class distinction and prejudice. As a representative of the Church, one whom they called later a "catalyst" pastor, I could get the economically divergent adult church members to mix and work together from conscience. But the same adults forbade the young people to mix. There was too much fear of intermarriage between economic classes. Strange, in a society where having a little black blood in you was viewed with pride like spice in your food, economic difference created enormous barriers. We have to learn to look and to respect more deeply.

*   *   *

Economic difference played its tune at full volume during the depression. One day a very wealthy friend from their school days visited my aunts next door. It may be worth noting, as we consider home and family, that she was the very first person I ever knew who had a divorce. She didn't impress me, but that enormous Rolls Royce! Head lights, fog lights, driving lights, parking lights, side signal flaps that lit, inside reading lights. I remember trying to count them and arguing with my brother about how many there were. This "have" was beyond all reach, but there it was in the driveway. But if Dad had owned a Rolls, would it have made a difference?

I often walked the mile to the country store to shop for Mom. Sometimes I had cash. Many times I asked them to charge it. The store owners did their best to carry many of the families in my home town during those harsh depression days. I imagine that most of their accounts were never paid. It was charitable and I am grateful, as I am sure many others are. But it was also in its own way demeaning. Well-meaning charity is too often misread as patronizing. While I respect the store owners to this day, sixty years later I still hate to use my credit cards. It's like saying "Charge it," at the country store.

My generation recouped much of its pride during the second great war, but from sad memory we cringe at "welfare" solutions. We've been on the receiving end and know how it feels. But our reaction can blossom into its own version of looking down on wealth. In our reverse prejudice, we are particularly prone to making it appear as if the wealth were unearned. Politicians for years have, for their own aggrandizement, irresponsibly pitted rich against poor, labor against management.

Such prejudicial reactions can begin very young and are a symptom of an immature faith. My wife came from an exceptionally wealthy family. I've been told a story about my wife's childhood. She came in response to a last minute bring-your-own lunch picnic. They had steak prepared for their big noon meal and so that's what she brought. In tears, this little girl begged to exchange her steak for the hot dog which her hostess was about to eat. That little girl who later became my wife passionately longed for economic normalcy. The love of money, not money itself, corrupts. Clearly the poor can be corrupted by the love of money and things as much as or sometimes even more than the rich. When a poor man daily yearns for a large screen television and a rich man simply goes out and buys two, with whom does the love of money do its worst?

One of my little nephews, when teased by his peers about his family's "millions", finally said, "The Lord gave my Grandfather money, and he gave it to us. Do you want to argue with the Lord?" Out of the mouth of babes! His mythical faith let him stand tall.

The association between racial prejudice and economic diversity often clouds the real issues. In our zeal for capitalism and its appropriate freedoms, we have foolishly allowed possessions to become the measure of human worth. Establishing and maintaining equal economic opportunity is a significant step to establishing a climate where prejudice can be overcome. Like civil order, sufficient wealth is a necessary foundation for justice. But economic programs which are mandated by law and fear of punishment undercut the individual human sense of personal integrity and worth. You can't compel genuine trust and respect. Too often we make the dream world of possessions into an idealized myth. Faith development flounders somewhere between disillusioned economic ideals and the real world of straining to get along with others. Those who do not have sufficiency wonder how they can ever fit into a society which continues to measure their worth only in dollars.

Internationally, our efforts to export capitalism to third world countries, even if well-intentioned and not exploitative, are not going to magically resolve the issues. And if we attempt to impose our economic solutions on them from a "better than thou" posture, they will not simply fail, they will be demeaning and destructive. Many emerging nations have a proud sense of the worth of the individual and of charitable responsibility to the greater family of society. In terms of human development, to a society which is striving to uphold a family sense of humanity what we offer often seems like a step backwards.

In a related economic issue, many of my African friends deeply resent the West's efforts to promote population control among them as our solution to their economic stress. They love children and family, and many of their beliefs are founded upon awe before the order of nature. They see our stance in racial terms, as an attempt to change the racial balance of the world's populations. This is particularly so when we expend more concern in limiting their populations than in limiting our own. While recently they have felt the pressure ease on promoting birth control, Africans are not stupid or deaf. They know that some racist whites are covertly saying that given time AIDS will take care of the problem in Africa. May God help us to grow beyond merely political or economic solutions to our human dilemma.

Colonialist economic exploitation kills trust, steals entrepreneurial delight, and lives on lies. The Volta dam, for example, was built ostensibly to help West Africa by providing cheap electricity and developing the bauxite in the region to manufacture aluminum. Now the electricity is still cheap, but the bauxite is imported from South America. The excuse: no infrastructure and inferior ore. What real economic benefit to Africa? Apparently, we didn't go there with the thought of what we could share. Instead we sought political power for the sake of controlling economic resources. We exploited. We didn't go to learn from their strengths, we went to change them into being like us. Now that Ghana is beginning to react against the injustices through economics, perhaps— but only perhaps—we will stop and think.

Such exploitation happened in Hawaii from both East and West. Earlier it happened with the native Americans in this country. While Hollywood treated us to its own version of how the West was won, perhaps a little reflection will show us what we could have learned.

Another example: In past days the missionaries descended on Africa. Given their sincerity, they nevertheless came with a message which divided our cultures for centuries. They pounded their Bibles and said, "Accept Christ and be saved, or you will all die in your sins." What more profoundly prejudicial stance can possibly be imagined than to say, "I am saved, you are eternally damned?" This was not just observing cultural or racial difference, this was a prejudicial claim as to the eternal destiny of human spirits. What is more, the judgment was attributed to God. Even the supposed simple animistic God of the tribes was bigger than that. I believe such an unjust a posture did and in some quarters is still doing untold harm to racial relations.

Some of the missionaries saw the love and the trust at the heart of the primitive communities. They said it was childlike. And it was childlike, but not childish. Love and trust preserved to maturity in grown men and women through a mythic ideal and conventional behavior are both precious and rare. Yet many from a posture of Western sophistication demeaned that faith and patronized—studied with fascination, but from on high with a Ph.D. as the goal. How much we could have learned had we only respected and loved these cultures! What we still can learn, though often we have been and still are our own worst enemies!

As the colonialists walked confidently in their supposed superiority as to religion, so they marched confidently in their assumed superiority as to politics, economics, and almost every other field that the social sciences have learned to explore.

These supposed learneds chose to see the resistance, the ferocity in tribal war, the harsh customs, and the severe religious rites and brand them all as heathen and barbaric. Even today it amuses me to hear TV commentators wax eloquent about how Somalia, Rwanda, or some other African nation has no government. Tribal governance may be eroding, but it is still a form of government and performs many governmental functions effectively. More often than not, the tribal chief acts in the name of God for the sake of human charity and brotherhood. Would that more of our leaders did. Most African tribal chiefs have the tacit if not the formal support of their people. If they get too far out of agreement with the common will as expressed by their councils, they can be removed.

I remember my first participation in the ceremony of the drinks to establish a lease of land from the local chief in Ghana. We brought two bottles of good European gin to a meeting with the chief and his council. The building was shabby and rundown. But the ceremony was pregnant with dignity. All knew English, but we communicated ceremonially through an "interpreter." After considerable discussion in the council in order to seal the agreement, the gin was opened. The chief then poured out a libation to the one great God and took a drink. The gourd cup was then passed to me, and unwittingly I did the same. There was something of a gasp, as I had not realized that previous Christian missionaries had refused to honor the great God in this way and to drink gin. With shock or wondering approval on the part of the chief and council, the deal went through. In discussing the transaction later, one of my African friends said, "Compare your contracts on paper to our verbal ones before the Great God. The memory of the Chief's Council will be passed from generation to generation, but your paper fades and rots." It's something to think about. It certainly happened with the native Americans.

The tragedy is that during the Cold War we and the Soviet Union provided armored cars and automatic weapons to replace the traditional clubs and spears in Somalia. We provided the weapons which turned tribal disagreements into conflagrations, and then had the gall to criticize the outcome.

Today we are eagerly exporting the supposed political, economic, and religious superiority of the West to the Far East. The balance of trade in material goods is in their favor, but I wonder how many recognize that the Far East is exporting more and more of its cultural and religious practices as well. Yoga, meditation technique, management techniques, acupuncture, herbal medicines, and diets are all being imported with great eagerness. And in the other direction we export traditional weddings with white wedding dresses, the latest videos, jeans and rock music. Who will benefit most from the social, cultural, and religious balance of trade?

There is a great need to revisit the history of colonialism, and not just for its influence in international relations. Often we as individuals are products of our natural attitudes and postures toward other cultures. America and Americans have reputations for conceit abroad which need sincere reexamination. Even if it were useful to determine whether our practices or our neighbor's were better, by what standard would we judge?

Many of us may say, "Leave that to the politicians—they're professionals at messing things up." But just as we reflect our country, our country reflects us. It is perhaps easier to look at some of our country's economic conceits than to see those same conceits applied by us to our neighbors next door. At first it may be easier to see the international power plays than to focus on the pressures and power struggles in our workplaces, in our neighborhoods, and even in our families.

These are not mature motivations. They need to be balanced, subordinated, and infilled, not with childhood's heroics, but with ideals tempered in the fires of life. If conventional behavior is to become worthy of the name "justice," we must look to it and beyond it honestly and faithfully. We must prune the rotten branches lest the rot beset the trunk itself. The solution out there must include the solution right here.

IV

▼

ACCEPTANCE—FREE OR FORCED
FROM CONVENTIONAL RULES TO
CONVENTIONAL FAITH

In later elementary school we had all the distorted Hollywood input. We shared the pictures from Esquire of women with mountainous breasts. We listened for and put our heads together over whatever dirty jokes we could glean.

Friday nights most of the girls in the upper elementary school babysat, while the adults went to a Church supper and Doctrinal Study. Though strictly forbidden, it was our opportunity to clandestinely go fraternize with the opposite sex. During these sessions,

I lost a portion of my naivete about the physical differences between the sexes. Given the circumstances, it still seems a miraculous Providential gift that I remained uninitiated into full sexual relations.

My friends would brag about their prowess and conquests. I would talk a similar exaggerated line. It was impossible to know what my friends really did. What were the checks? Traditional respect for girls? Beginning conscience? Fear of parental discovery? Who knows what put my brakes on. But what a blessing to avoid the physical exploitation of another human being for the sake of self-gratification, or even experimentation. More than that, what a wonderful world of mutual discovery was saved for marriage—a truly special set of rewards saved in order to honor one unique person of the opposite sex.

As our early elementary years pass, our behavior and attitudes move from society's explicit to its implicit instruction. While still conventionalized, they change from first being on the say-so of parents and teachers to being based on the pressure of peers. From imposed rules they become internalized as a conventional moral code. A kind of traditional faith based on the say-so of others rationalizes our former mythical ideals. This faith may or may not become functional in determining our daily lives, but it is part of the equation. It calls for such things as justice, integrity, and honor. It is this faith which probably saved me in those dark rooms on Friday nights. On the other hand, caring what my peers thought led to the vividly imagined details I told my friends.

At this stage our growing moral values are determined essentially by the modeling and the say-so of others. The idols of our myths give way to heroic peers. Our faith is not really thought through or acted upon as our own. But it does allow us to rediscover our sense of belonging in an expanded human community. The challenge is to win a place there. That place may be in a distorted and limited clique of special friends or it may be open to a much broader human scene. Rules, role models, and peers all contribute to our growing conventional value system. Conventional faith need not be the traditional values of a previous generation. Whatever form it takes, its limitation is that it owes its allegiance to the opinion of others, usually parents succeeded by peers.

In the context of this developing conventional faith it is interesting to look at the public school classroom teacher who cannot teach religious values. Picture a first grade teacher's dilemma when a child innocently asks, "Who made me?" Today we are confronted with a public school system which in the name of separation of church and state insists upon trying to be religious-value neutral. But we cannot function together with others without human value judgments. Perhaps the best example of this self-imposed school policy is teaching sex education as if it were a plumbing course based on physical experience alone. You can give students condoms and tell them how to use them, but without disclosing your values what can you say about why or why not to use them other than perhaps the risk of disease? If our moral principles are determined simply by our fears or adaptation to the group in which we find ourselves, how do they apply when we find ourselves in new and very different groups?

The car, for example, can allow teenagers to escape in a few minutes from any parental or community observance. They are freed from fear of adult sanctions and to a large extent from any direct peer influence. A driver's license and free use of a car involves far more than safety on the highway. It involves responsible behavior in the back seat. Teens are frequently constrained as much by the situation in which they find themselves as by the rules they have been taught. When my parents required a chaperone if we went out in mixed company in a car, we found a chaperone who openly said that he would keep his eyes on the road and not us. Yet the fact that he was there provided some boundaries. In retrospect I think my parents knew the limitations of our chosen chaperone, but also knew the checks provided even through minimal adult presence.

But when the goal of our faith becomes adapting to different circumstances and winning acceptance, it in fact prevents the development of that faith beyond the level of conventional behavior. Adaptation to others is the foundation of conventional behavior. Acceptance and friendship emerge as top priorities. Unfortunately, the faith of a great many stalls at this very point of simply getting along. Thus we observe that many today are "experts" at making quantities of shallow friends, but find it almost impossible to share the more profound human feelings and concerns which feed friendship in depth. Overcoming prejudice and really understanding diversity can never stop at simple and shallow adaptation. Real friendship requires the depth and closeness of discovering the shared values of our common humanity.

Democratic theory argues against having special groups—though politicians often achieve their power through manipulating special interests, even pitting one group against another. In the classroom, shunning cliques and accepting everybody indiscriminately often becomes the teacher's ideal. By denying discriminating value judgments they are denying the opportunity to freely and confidently give trust and love to others.

At the same time that moral and spiritual concepts are minimized, the amount of data an elementary school student absorbs is amazing. But data does not determine values nearly so much as does interaction with a group. Most early friendships are born at school. While we may learn good study and work habits through reading, writing, and arithmetic, many of childhood's values are confirmed on the school buses, in the halls, and on the playgrounds. We choose our peer heroes. They become the leaders, and their conventional values and behavior challenge the traditional faith we got at home.

For years, Dewey-inspired, we developed democratic classrooms throughout the country. "New" teaching methods sprang from a wide variety of applications of democratic group process. Kids ran mini-Washingtons in the classroom, with much less bureaucracy than the real thing in D.C. Learning groups were "un-prejudicially" divided into bluebirds or cardinals, but we all knew what they meant. A pragmatic notion of what made the group "work" was adopted. We were preparing the whole person for the "real world." But if normative behavior is determined by a democratic process, it is not hard to see that the majority of our peers determine the moral outcome—i.e. conventional faith. And in a Dewey classroom, that faith is always relative. Justice rests upon conventional faith, but genuine justice reaches far beyond civil law and moral rules even to absolutes. Without a higher law, how can you or I protect against the injustice of the very society itself in which we live?

Fortunately, the "real" democratic society for which we were preparing students was not so stringently curtailed regarding moral values as the school classroom has become. Our forefathers made some basic assumptions, such as that all men are created equal and from their Creator have certain inalienable rights. Constitutional government demands not just loyalty to civil law, covering overt actions, but also to a law which demands such things as basic human justice under God. Our forefathers knew that without such values you cannot break out of conventional behavior and still maintain responsibility to others. They tried to walk a line condemning the idea of a state religion but encouraging a religious state. You really cannot sustain a constitutional democracy without acknowledging the God-given natural moral rights of others. It is one thing freely to respect the minorities because it is God's will. But it is demeaning and prejudicial if respect pragmatically becomes simply a matter of civil law as the most effective way to manage and control our relation to each other. Society can impose a change of actions upon us, but only

God can change our hearts. Honoring
diversity demands a change of heart.

Our heart, our ruling or dominant love,
determines our purpose in life and its course.
We cultivate this love according to what we
believe to be good, or according to the principles we believe define the human being we
should strive to become. When we genuinely
respect and love another, it is not an imposed
obligation but a freely bestowed gift of the
spirit. Conventions cannot legislate such
things as respect and love or thought and
will, but our individual understanding of our
relationship to God can. God reveals what we
believe true humanity and human rights
should be. An adequate belief concerning
humanity fosters individual freedom as the
key to individual love. It goes to the heart and
protects others from us as much as it protects
us from others. The highest human and loving relationship is between a person and his
God. The struggle for human rights must
reach to this level or human relationships
cannot fully come to trusting closure in freedom of choice. Religious freedom is one of
those precious human rights. Religious diversity manifested in life is a logical outcome of
such freedom under God.

In an orderly state the atheist has an
absolute right to think and will what he
pleases about religion, but he does not have
the right to speak and act overtly against

religion, because to do so is an attack against the other's freedom to reach beyond conventional values. We uphold the right of inquiry for an agnostic who expresses doubt in speech and action. But an atheist should not have the right to publicly attack what others see as the way to a deeper humanity. Doubt allows freedom of inquiry and religious choice; denial shuts it down.

Our forefathers saw that a state-sponsored religion was wrong because it allowed the collective power of the state to impose its values on the individual citizen. They knew that civil law is enforced by fear of punishment. A state religion makes religion merely conventional, allowing the power of the majority a superior position to the individual religious conscience. It simply does not protect individual faith and freedom of religion. From the perspective of conventional control, it is interesting to reflect on the low percentages of attendance and commitment to state religion in those countries which sponsor it.

But moral law is enforced by society through the threat of the loss of reputation, honor, or gain. Reputation, honor, and gain are often awarded or withheld through the collective or commonly accepted opinion of the majority. Moral law is still conventional. But under moral law any of us can respect and love our neighbor freely as a matter of conscience despite society's opinion. If we do so believing it is the will of an omnipresent God, then that respect and love can rise above relativism, above legislation, above coercion or convention. When God enters, we take responsibility before Him as individuals.

In contrast, as society tries to reconcile the majority to the minority, it calls for compromise and shades of gray. But not so conscience. So far as the individual establishes a human relationship with his God, his value system will become fixed and absolute, and he will treasure human rights wherever and whenever he comes in contact with another human being. A truly religious life reaches out freely to others. Genuine love is either given or withheld as a free choice.

When we feel prejudice then, that feeling is not based simply on the overt actions of others or society. Prejudices hurt because we assume that they spring from attitudes of thought and deliberate will. We grieve because they seem to be choices from the core of people's being and intention. The real hurt is the alienation of the spirit. It takes individual conscience to control those attitudes of thought and will and change them into genuinely human acceptance. In short, prejudice runs much deeper than the hateful words and deeds that the civil laws of the majority can control through fear of punishment. We want to be respected for who we are, not because someone is compelled by law to act decently towards us. If the greater part of society subscribes to human fairness, it may through moral pressure be able to prevent unfair practice wherever the majority opinion prevails. But it will still not satisfy the deep yearning for acceptance from love. Real change will only come when we see our diversity as created by God, and in the full freedom of conscience accept each other because each of us has the potential to be a member of His eternal human kingdom.

Traditions and conventions pave the way, for order is the basis of free choice. But nations which stall at conventional values are truly nations at risk.

I have a Korean friend, here in America, whose father died when he was a boy. I am deeply touched by his choosing to honor me as a special older person in his life. Something profound happens when he makes a special trip to give me a gift—or calls long distance on special days.

Again, when one of my former Korean parishioners was transferred, he went fully to the carpet to bow in a more traditional farewell after we shook hands. I was embarrassed and touched at the same time.

I believe more is involved than keeping the mats clean when you remove your shoes on entering an oriental person's house. It honors his home. We may smile as we see two orientals bow to each other, but there are countless acts of respect and honor which are built into their traditional culture. Many of our discussions and decisions have turned as much on points of honor as on lines of reason. Honor is traditionally worth fighting, even dying for. It is a strong conventional yet moral precept in that culture.

I have observed Japanese and Koreans as their traditions are challenged. Little by little, through the impact of waves of Western culture, erosion has taken place, subtle at first, but rising almost to Sunami proportions. Traditional civil and moral values are needed to preserve order until the values of a higher conscience of the spirit take over. The percentage of Japanese who have accepted the Christian religion is still measured in low single digits. I wonder what percent wear western clothes, play "our" music, or have adopted our habit of measuring human worth in dollars or yen.

In Asia as elsewhere tension always develops between parent and child as an adolescent struggles to become himself. Hairstyles, clothing, makeup, diet, all the social conventions are challenged. Walk a street in Tokyo or spend a week in a Japanese or Korean home, and you will see evidence of this just as you see it on our streets. I have seen East and West come together in the new generation in oriental homes, in their society, and in their church. At times it reminds me of occluded fronts in a weather system—and I watch for tornadoes.

In a similar way immigrants face a cultural shock that shakes their conventional faith and creates a tremendous fear. Trying to overcome that fear from below involves compromise at best—and usually threatens strongly rooted traditions. The greatest hope is to solve it from above by uncovering a common humanity which only religious conviction can define. But how are we to do this?

We tried to mix first generation Korean-American and American children in the same Sunday School. The children all spoke beautiful English, even though their parents still struggled. Language was not the problem. But in many cases Korean parents simply could not expose their children to the easygoing and sometimes disrespectful attitudes of the American kids. Jeans and even hairstyles they might accept, but not behavior which challenged the very framework of their homes and culture. We were trying to move too quickly and too far. They might have been at home in a nineteenth century classroom, but not in today's.

It is interesting that individualized classrooms are now replacing the democratically inspired classrooms of the past. Groups of birds have been replaced by individual snowflakes or flowers, each learning at its own pace. This change in the instructional environment can be seen in developmental terms as an effort to break out of the bonds of merely conventional faith. It remains to be seen if this change becomes simply an existential effort to "become" by pushing away from all societal norms, or if it will open the door to a religious renewal in education. Self-realization, if the self be a true and God-given one, is reaching for a vision—far more than pushing away.

During the Vietnam War many asserted their individualism by protesting our country's policies and particularly the draft. Much of rebellion and escape remains in the succeeding "drug" culture. Traditional values are mocked in music, in the media, and in behavior. Almost every profession has been denigrated: doctors, lawyers, ministers, politicians, you name it. A generation found much to be against but little to be for. And now its members are trying to figure out what to do with their adolescent kids. Our nation is starving for values which will restore responsibility and respect in society. Yet traditional values in many cases are justifiably seen as having too much imposed baggage and as too "unreal" to win loyalty. We've been there; done that.

In this climate, police patrol the halls of many public schools to maintain order. Learning demands order, and in its beginnings, obedience and self-control are upheld through fear. But faith matures as the child moves from obeying those in authority to being led by group values and role models, to obeying commonly accepted rules, until his own will is voluntarily restrained for the sake of others. It is a strange and frightening thing to have educators advocate teaching the whole child, and yet rule out instruction which would nourish and nurture a growing individual conscience. To have young people suffering spiritual malnutrition while society counts only on the fear of civil law to control them is nothing short of tragic.

Public schools today may study and debate civil rights. On the basis of constitutional rights they may even try to encourage reflection on moral issues and societal attitudes. But without God they cannot lead much beyond conventional behavior. They can raise questions. They may encourage individual reflection and "values clarification." But the only "answer" they can express is a collective and reflective relativism. When it comes to prejudice, this is at best a partial or beginning basis for an answer. In terms of developmental faith the simple truth is that, as defined by law today, our public schools cannot provide a real and lasting answer to prejudice, nor can they lead to a humanly effective way to handle diversity.

Certainly some of the private and even parochial schools have an agenda of separate education which is racially offensive. Still other religious schools take a posture of a human authoritarianism, which also stifles the growth of individual faith. But a great many private schools envision an education which encourages a maturation of faith that simply is not possible in the public setting any more. Many parents who espouse home schooling despite its demanding challenges hold similar ideals. Only a mature faith can bring the battle against prejudice to the heart. Religion must not only allow for, but even provide for the free and responsible maturation of faith whether in religious schools or in the churches themselves. For all the talk that says we need affections in order to learn, it is somewhat surprising that we do not seem to recognize that God gives us the ability to be affected and to love. He alone provides the basis for all human relationships.

As the products of our schools move into the workplace, management too has gone through an adjustment. First, participative management emerged, focussing on winning the support of the employees by using committees. It was frankly an attempt to resolve the tension between labor and management through a unique use of democratic compromise. In many cases the appearance of participation far exceeded the reality. Many middle managers left because the bosses could not really delegate. Culturally, a wave of individualism was asserting itself for which participative management is at best an incomplete answer—and at worst offends the minority on a day-by-day basis in the workplace. Job mobility and the assertion of the individual now more and more challenged the tools of conventional management. This is just one more place where the individual is attempting to rise above conventional ways and yet does not see clearly how to avoid radical individualism and work with others. Sincere, just and faithful performance in the workplace as a matter of conscience is often very rare.

A similar challenge has confronted the institution of marriage. For years, drawing on common religious roots, the conventions of society upheld it as a covenant for life. But today counselors use the tools of compromise and even suggest managing homes on a democratic model. Some even reduce sexual relations from an act expressive of love to a scientifically derived physical manipulation. Under the guise of freedom, which was really misguided license, our civil and moral conventions have gradually made divorce respectable. This posture is now reinforced by the assertion of the individual rights of husband and wife. The beautiful root meaning of covenant as a free coming together for a mutual benefit is too often being thought of as a commitment to a contract which, if it doesn't "work out," can be abandoned or broken.

So in our schools, at work, in our homes—in fact across our whole culture—the individual is pushing out against convention. Fowler describes this in terms of a movement toward a fourth stage of development, Individuative-Reflective faith. "Individuative-reflective faith is particularly critical for it is in this transition that the late adolescent or adult must begin to take seriously the burden of responsibility for his or her own commitments, lifestyle, beliefs and attitudes. Where genuine movement toward stage 4 is underway the person must face certain unavoidable tensions: individuality versus being defined by a group or group membership; subjectivity and the power of one's strongly felt but unexamined feelings versus objectivity and the requirement of critical reflection; self-fulfillment or self-actualization as a primary concern versus service to and being for others; the question of being committed to the relative versus struggle with the possibility of an absolute."[2]

---

2 Fowler, p. 182

In my case, this struggle lasted throughout adolescence and had no clearly defined turning point. But the questions about conventional rules began to build in late elementary school and were associated with an early choice of a career.

In fifth grade a minister came to our school and gave a talk on his work. He traveled all around the country visiting in individual homes, giving worship, and teaching people about the Lord. He caught my imagination. His work sounded important and exciting. He was not exactly the hero type, but somehow I decided that I wanted to be a minister. Perhaps it wasn't so strange to decide what I wanted to be at that age. What was strange is that the decision stuck and gradually led to a career focussed on service to others.

At the end of sixth grade I was moved into a public school in a small Wisconsin city. The depression was just ending, and Dad's newfound work called him away from the church community. I saw it as a surrender of his values. All my life he had stressed the value of socializing within the church group. Now we were going by his choice to a place where I knew no one, and where no one had the same religious values he had taught me were so important. This erosion of his role in my life was further confirmed by going with him on a sales trip and overhearing his telling dirty stories to one of his customers.

He had always punished me for this; how could he do it?

I had been trained to expect open evil. Coming from a very small denomination, I also expected that no one would appreciate or understand my values. When I asked myself can the rest of the world be wrong, my childish answer was, "Yes." Now, this also included my family who had turned their backs on their principles. I was betrayed. I never felt so alone. At every opportunity I would go fishing in the river by myself or play endlessly in my room.

I can remember when we visited home and I would go to church, I simply could not hold back the tears when we said the Lord's prayer. The cause was much more than homesickness. It may have been because of my age at the time. My brother, only a year and a half older, even ran for student council in junior high. Whatever the reason, I had been given an ideal that fed a prejudice toward those not of our religion that I could not handle at first. I was a religious minority, and from fear I held back from accepting either my parents or my peers. I was striving prematurely to be an individual.

I remember hearing the devastating news of Pearl Harbor one Sunday morning while we were in Wisconsin. I could not really feel the shock, but from then on every soldier, sailor, marine, or pilot became my hero. December seventh unleashed everything heroic in my imagination. As I played with my lead soldiers—gray Germans, brown for Allies—I identified with the war. I led the troops through the jungles against Japan. I raced my tanks, touch and go against the Germans' best in the desert, and I mockingly defeated the Italians. For me and at least half a generation around me who followed the exploits of those who actually fought, that stupendous war molded our love of country in a unique and profound way.

It altered our lives too. After two years in Wisconsin we returned to our hometown. With the fickleness of a child, I had eventually acquired a couple of "Wisconsin" friends who were not so bad. And my parents' decision to return "home" proved they too were almost OK.

Young as we were, the war made its demands on us. We filled in with part-time jobs. During the school year I worked in a drug store. I was supposed to only jerk sodas, but when we got busy I worked the cigarette and sometimes the drug counter. To this day I can still feel the embarrassment of the first time I was asked for condoms and I did not know what they were.

I got to know some of the girls who came in for ice cream. One night I was late getting home, and Dad came out looking, saw me with them, and later accused me falsely of necking. I'll never know if he exaggerated to caution and shame me, or if he really believed his accusations. While his influence was still there, that incident was one more step towards breaking his conscious influence on my life. "You can make me do things, but I'll think and feel whatever I want," I thought.

Most of the laborers went off to the war. A local nursery had no help to hoe weeds or pick the cash crop of tomatoes. They paid us by the bushel for the tomatoes because we spent so much time throwing the rotten ones at each other. The squishier they were, the harder to throw. But what satisfaction when they hit! Hoeing was much harder. I had had blisters before, but not like these. When we slowed up, the boss would come out and "Show us how." He'd go like a roto-tiller for five or ten minutes and then go back into the office. There was one laborer in his high shoes and bib overalls who in a strange way was one of us. He was too old for the war. I have always appreciated how he taught us to pace ourselves.

Being so young, we worked only six hours a day. They were both long and proud hours. When I had to apply for a social security card, I was grown up. But I still smarted over the thought of the government's planning to take care of me fifty years later. It was my first brush with the impact of social legislation's trying to take away my responsibility to be myself. I wanted so much to take care of myself and to hold my head up. Who were they anyway? What did they know? I still believe that government social legislation usually demeans the individual and stunts the growth of character. In developmental terms, dependency holds back thinking for oneself and the human blessings of responsible human choice. I believe the reaction against politics and government is often driven by the human desire to somehow be an individual. The challenge is to be an individual and at the same time be responsible to and serve others.

In late elementary school, with the help of a couple of fathers, we began a Boys Club. Naturally, one of the first challenges was to raise money. So we all burned cork and blackened our faces, and the annual Boys Club Minstrel Show was born. We sang the old sentimentalities with strident enthusiasm. The jokes were pitiful, along the line of those of the then popular "Black Crows." I don't know why I can't remember any of them. Costumes and makeup were the way out of self-consciousness. We were more into pretending than anything very specific about pretending to be blacks. But we did poke fun and make them appear Uncle Tom. I think all the slow, dumb, lazy stereotypes were at the very least subliminally present. But mostly we had costumes. We got laughs, probably more at than with us. We earned money. We loved it. I could play a "nigger" on the stage, even though my Mom would never let me say the word. Our notions about blacks were somewhat confirmed in a totally unreal way. Ethnic jokes reinforce conventional prejudices.

I am sure that there is a line between harmless and harmful ethnic jokes. But, as with sarcasm, both the initiator and the listener need to have the same line. Some of the best Jewish stories I have ever heard were told by Jews on themselves. But I don't feel I should tell them. Individual conscience says "No."

The war provided all kinds of "Ah So" Japanese jokes. Of course we learned the words to Spike Jones' "Der Fuhrer's Face." Newsreels of Bob Hope's visits to the soldiers added still more material. Movies à la "Hogan's Heroes" also filled in the humor. But when the Japanese were moved from the West Coast and took away our hoeing jobs, it was no joke. So much is written about the impact of the war on the generation that served, and rightly so. But we who followed immediately behind were affected powerfully too.

Years later I walked to the top of a hill in Okinawa with one of our Church leaders. He was my age, part of the generation following. As we looked out at the blue Pacific waters breaking on the shore, he looked up at the sky and said, "I remember sitting here and watching your dive bombers coming in from over there." The war, the lead soldiers, the mocking jokes, even the deaths of some we loved were almost in another world. The two of us saw the Pacific with our eyes and felt peace in our hearts. We found human closeness in our shared religious values, and the dead were almost buried.

While those serving had lots of experience with the Japanese as enemies and the blacks as companions, we boys back home had almost no experience of either. Our attitudes were simply shaped by what we were told. I suspect that the lack of real human experience with blacks is part of the reason why many find it convenient to ignore the problem. If you have never had to meet an issue, it is easier to ignore it than to think it through and act on your convictions. Even today I still have moments when I would like to get rid of racial issues by letting someone else pick up the problem. But somehow late childhood put in my heart an underlying sense of fairness. I could say it was the blacks' problem, but it just doesn't work. Something is in there that says, "No." Thanks, Mom.

I wish that I had grown up knowing some black children my age, but I am certainly glad that my biggest media influence was a radio set shaped in the form of a Gothic arch at Grandma's house. I had to go to Grandma's to hear it, and it always seemed to be tuned to the news or "One Man's Family," or some other dumb program. I could tinker with the sputter on my crystal set. Sometimes at night under the covers, supposedly asleep, I could listen to "The Shadow." We may not have been broadly media experienced, but as I listen to some of the restored radio tapes, like the hammers of a piano they strike again the old chords of attitudes I thought were forgotten. "The Black Crows" or Jack Benny's Rochester are incongruous in today's attitudes. But clearly the radio shaped many of my prejudices, though not so profoundly as the media today. Many of today's lyrics are disgustingly demeaning of women in ways our generation never would have thought possible. *Esquire* may have distorted my view of women's shapes, but today's films in the specious name of realism manipulate the relation between the sexes until actually walking in a red light district looks pretty tame by comparison. I am so tired of murder mysteries, international intrigues, and even the human tangles in science fiction all being solved in bed. I wish I could be encouraged to buy beer just because it tasted good. Even the news media seem to be trying more and more to shape experience rather than simply to report it. We don't go out and plan to be prejudiced. But our experience shapes our conscious and unconscious.

Even though we are unaware of the impact of our childhood experiences at the time, I believe that we really have to revisit our past in order to know ourselves. We need to see the distortions, hear the subtle play on feelings, smell the rotten attitudes, and have taste revolted again. We have to go back and sample some of those awful things again, because in so many hidden ways they shape our present attitudes. Then perhaps, if we really care, we can begin to put the influence of the media into a more balanced perspective.

As I write of more and more recollections of things of which I am less than proud, I realize that revisiting the possible origins of our prejudices is a messy task. It is too easy to blame our society or our past for who we are today. But if we are still victims of others, we have not realized our true potential as individuals. We need to examine ourselves in depth in the light of right and wrong to effect any useful growth and change. The baby has to be changed if ever it is to smell clean. Such self-examination must of necessity be done largely in our own homes, even our own closets. It is our work, not society's.

Growth is a strange combination of natural exploration and controlled experiences. But sooner or later our conscious focus shifts from simple affectional responses to questioning. Our morals don't need forced feeding and growth hormones, but we can't take real responsibility until we begin to understand the issues. Reality must be there. But reality involves thoughts and feelings as well as words and deeds.

A tremendous amount of prejudice is molded and sustained by conventional norms. When we step on a bus and see an open seat by a black and one by a white, we may need to stop and think about our instinctive choice. Still, for all its limitations, let us not forget that conventional faith is a necessary precursor to individual faith. It establishes and maintains the basic order in which choice is possible. You can't back up and think in a chaotic world. We need the constants of convention in order to declare who we are, to say "yes" or "no" to being like others or aspiring to revealed values which we believe to be true whether others accept them or not. Think back. Do you see growth and change? Are you taking charge and working through those pre-established patterns of youth? Or when it comes to the opposite sex, to races, or any other differences, are you still responding to the same tunes you danced to in high school?

V

On My Own

Faith as an Individual Choice

The elementary school Principal insisted that under no circumstances would she recommend my going to the Church's boarding school in Pennsylvania. Still, I was admitted. I don't know whether the school didn't pay attention to her or whether she was just trying to scare me. I thought I disliked, even hated her with her little pince-nez tweaking her nose. But at the same time I respected her and knew she stood for what was right.

The thousand-mile train ride. There's still something romantic to me about the smell of coal smoke. Bumming a ride from the old brown electric-train-style station sitting beside its single track; seeing for the first time the ivy-covered school dormitory; carrying those heavy suitcases one more time up three flights of steps; smelling the fresh coat of paint on the beat-up walls; looking for my name on a card on the door. Each detail enhanced the anticipation. I was on my own.

At fifteen, I was delighted with the thought of being away from home. One part of me said I could break with home rules and do what I wanted. The other knew that I myself needed to take charge and change. I soon realized that the dormitory had its own complete set of rules even stricter than Mom's. They gave me something to complain about and to test. They also gave me something to accept as my own.

My best friend was younger and would remain at home for another year. We had plagued the girls together and spent hours discussing them. We had delightedly shared dirty jokes and dirty pictures. We had dumped garbage cans together on Halloween and stayed three steps ahead of the homeowners who chased us. All of it was fun, but in my heart I knew that our being separated was good. With him it was fast and easy, but so much of it was dumb. I knew that on my own I would give up some of the crud we shared. It was hard—very hard—but underneath it was right. He was a peer I could do without. I needed to become myself. Yet, boy did I want to find someone to fill the void, to be accepted and to belong, in my new class, in the dorm, in the fraternity, among new friends.

Many of the girls from home had come to the same parochial school as I did. I naively thought that I could put my past behind me! But reputation is like a soft lump of clay in the hands of adolescent girls. I didn't know the whispered warnings about how fast I was that were circulating in the girls' dorm. I didn't see the heads together and the curious looks my way. Not knowing freed me from past pressure and gave me a chance to become myself in a new setting. Somehow I began to establish a new name. The new set of peers, particularly in the boy's dorm, made starting over easier. They either weren't in the loop or didn't care.

My assigned roommate was from Canada. He had a record player, played classical music of all things, and had a funny accent. We teased him for saying "Abaoot." Everyone called the students from Canada "Black Canadians." It was sort of traditional to look down on the "Canooks" as dumb. They sneaked off campus and smoked. But *we* were athletes. Only when the school started a hockey team that winter did we realize how athletic *they* were. Had dorm tradition had its way, there would have been a gulf between me and my roommate, but he too was making a new start, and desperate to belong. Somehow our need for acceptance cut through the well-established teen prejudices. We formed a barbershop quartet together with two others. Later we went to college together. We even went to theological school together and are still so close that whenever our work or chance brings us together we just pick up conversations wherever we left off.

I wanted to stand up for something, though I didn't really know yet what it was. A few things about my past I knew were wrong. But I was also looking for something that really counted. In retrospect the process was pretty shallow. But that was the way I began to break out of the box my peers and I had made for me back home.

The dorm was all noise. Running. Shouting. Slugging. Seniors "helping us feel at home," with snickering laughs. I wanted so much to be "cool," but inside I was sweating. I didn't know what went and what didn't. It was a far deeper and more important challenge to my values than I realized at the time. I wasn't me yet.

The school knew us in some ways better than we knew ourselves. They presented what counted and then let us inquire into our religion in living terms. It gave us a set of principles outside of ourselves, God-given principles, one of the first of which was that if you want to be free you must take responsibility. Will peers determine our values or will freely accepted values determine us? Man-made dogma or imposed Church organizations are just conventional forces. They can't set you free from conventional bonds. God alone can teach you how to be yourself in such a way that you can be truly human to others, freely because He wants it so.

We had turned in our ration books at the "Bean Hall." School rules said we should call it the "Dining Hall." School rules said a lot of things. They could be challenged, and were. But not the Ten Commandments. They stood.

The food was food, but just. The Bean Hall manager always seemed to run out of ration stamps at the end of every month. So we went meatless. The coffee trained me for life to tolerate anything in a cup. The manager dithered while we looked at cold macaroni. The whole setup gave us ample chance to strut and complain with our peers. But something independent was stirring too.

I thought I was breaking out. I bounced against the rules, doubted, questioned. Somehow the authorities knew where I was and were one step ahead. They were consciously training me for freedom with responsibility towards others. Several of the teachers were role models, respected and accessible to guide and advise. The school employed no professional counselor. We had caring and available adults instead. They did not have to fear a lack of parental support, still less liability suits. All of the teachers took responsibility for their students, not just for their subject matter.

Today I wonder if, for all the emphasis on professionalism, things are subtly changing. Is the school somehow more concerned with self-realization than self-control? One of our recent high school students told me, "The problem with the high school is that it says the Church has all the answers when it should say that the Lord has." What a beautiful way of expressing the necessary transition from group organizational values to an individual responsibility to God.

There were two blacks on campus, the cook and the janitor. Both were institutions. Our paths crossed when we did student work sweeping floors, emptying trash, etc. The janitor sort of supervised us, sometimes reported our goofing off, but mostly just kidded around and cleaned the bathrooms. It was just the way things were, but it registered. Later when I worked on the summer painting crew and the janitor was my "boss," I learned he had a terrific sense of humor, was a pretty good handyman, and knew a lot about politics and life in general. He became a real person, not just a fixture. We still talked him down as a boss, but just like the boss at the nursery or drug store or anywhere else, not because of his color.

My church's doctrines are not WASP. Most churches' aren't. But somehow we turned out WASP. A subtle human dimension won out over unspoken doctrinal teachings. I've wondered about that unintended subtlety of evil so many times. When I asked my teachers why there were no black students, I was told that forty years ago some blacks from South Africa had come to school. But "It hadn't worked." To make them feel more comfortable, the Africans were quartered in the basement of the Bean Hall instead of in the dorm with the rest of the students. I thought to myself, "Yeah, the bishop at the time was a Southerner." So many assumptions about race are simply justification of the status quo. Acquired attitudes, unconscious baggage, unintentional habits, the very things I was wrestling with in other aspects of my life, made me wonder. I questioned, but the issue wasn't my focus either. It took years for the question to really grow within me until it became an un-lanced boil.

I played football in high school. One of the opposing schools had one seemingly endless family of blacks. The same family name popped up on the sports teams for about twenty years. They were from the one truly integrated school in the league, and they were the best halfbacks we ever played. Fast? I'll tell you they were. I think a couple of them later made the pros. I played line, and often I couldn't get a hand on them. They were too quick, and snakey as well. The truth was that they were better than I was, much better. It made me mad, and yet I had to admire them. I knew inside that they were better, but I covered for it in the locker room, "Did you notice how those black guys smell? Whew, they're so sweaty and slippery you can't tackle them." How could I voice the admiration that I really felt and still be a part of the team? I was ambivalent as heck, but strangely never really felt that I was mixed up.

About this time, sweeping racial generalities crept into our conversations. Not only did blacks smell. Blacks weren't very bright. Or blacks were just emotional. I was convinced that if a black really wanted to, he could make it big in athletics. Obviously they all didn't, so they must be lazy. On the other hand I was forced to admit, even if not publicly or even consciously, that while I was good at some things, some people were better, and some of them were black. It was only football, and I had plenty of public excuses, but I knew. It is hard to admit our limitations, but it is a first step towards becoming ourselves. Are they boundaries or limitations? Either humility or conceit can set us apart from others. But humility wins the long-term respect of others.

Humility shared between races or between the sexes! What a thought!

At the time, black athletes were emerging in the major professional sports, but they were not nearly the heroes some are today. Our first heroes often become role models for our early idealistic conventional behavior. But depending on where we are, rebel heroes whose main purpose is to stand out from the crowd may supersede. It may take an existential thrust of will to break with conventions, but it takes a commonly shared vision to really lead. Few adolescents know which will win. With time and real work we can discover that to be our hero a person must stand up for what we believe is right. But it takes years of sorting—changing friendships—testing boundaries—mistakes.

Some people try to make a big thing of the fact that blacks have broken into professional athletics. They suppose this will help their sense of racial pride. But when white sports heroes play only a limited role as models in the white community, is it realistic to expect athletic heroes from the black community to somehow symbolize and epitomize the emergence of black racial significance? Increasingly, black writers and educators too are emerging as leaders in individual reflection, and particularly beginning to break out of the party-line political power struggles and imposed solutions. But again, their existential cry against the injustice of the system may set the stage, but in and of itself it will not provide the vision for a solution. As a result of O.J. Simpson's trial, many called for a dialogue, particularly as it relates to the disparate views that whites and blacks have of our justice system. Such a dialogue could perhaps help each side see where the other is coming from and why. But the usual "visionary" antidote to conventional abuses is some political action or government program. Calling attention to the abuses may lead to some civil reforms, but if or when it slips into the political arena, where power is the name of the game, it cannot rise above imposed solutions. Such solutions simply don't reach deep enough to inspire the genuine acceptance of human variety.

I was in my middle teens when the men came home from the Second World War. They had won. They were heroes. Or were they? Certainly they had defended our country. But they came back changed. I'm glad I can't trace it to any individual, but somehow I picked up the message that black women were better in bed than white. It was the "in the know" stuff that teen-aged boys trade with each other like the sexy magazine pictures they hide under their mattresses. Since this was based on the experience of white servicemen, and not on racially mixed marriages, it was pretty clear that love, friendship and respect were not part of "being better." Still the idea just sort of remained in there. It had a strange way of popping up when I took a glance at *Ebony*, saw a movie, or perhaps just someone walking by on the street. I didn't put out a welcome mat for the thoughts, but still I wondered.

I was fascinated years later in a Ghanaian hotel to be talking to a Belgian businessman over breakfast. I had had dinner with him and his wife a few nights before she returned to Europe. He explained that the reason I had seen him with a black prostitute the night before was that he simply had to find out for himself whether, "Black women were better in bed." His conclusion? "How stupid he was."

On the same visit to Ghana, I got acquainted with a black tennis pro at the hotel. As we sat by the courts one day he said, "You know, someone is trying to kill me. Not the way you think, with a knife or anything. He has placed something from the medicine doctor on the court that is supposed to gradually take away my strength. My minister said that if I prayed the magic would have no effect." He then recited one of the Psalms and earnestly asked, "Do you think that will work?" His loyalty was divided between the witch doctor of the past and the Christian minister of the present. He was caught between two cultures that were fighting it out in his head. His roots, his mystical beliefs as well as many of his conventions, said one thing, yet he wanted to believe another. Knowing the power of his former beliefs, with some trepidation I told him that the Psalm would work. There is a lot of reversion in first generation conversion. Today cultures overlap and mix, often superficially, but the core from their earliest developmental life holds fast.

Over in Korea and Japan, bewildered oldest sons pleaded with me, "I no longer believe in worshiping ancestors, yet my family's integrity depends upon my leading in honoring my ancestors. What shall I do?" I know just how much the law and convention concerning the family is the glue for their culture, and I search for an answer. How do they break out?

From spurious superiority, we tend to ridicule the arranged marriages that still take place in some cultures. But most of those marriages last for life. Compare their statistics with those of our culture, where so many treat sexual relations like clothing. If you like it and it fits, keep it; if not, put it back on the rack for someone else. Is it simply from defensiveness that when cultures meet, both seem to feel they must claim superiority? Often the seeming depth and conviction of their defense is nothing more than protecting their own conventional behavior and beliefs.

The Japanese immigration department is said to readily issue working permits to

American women who plan to work as barmaids or give English instruction. It's superficial, but one of the apparent driving forces is the Japanese men's fascination with the size of American women's breasts. It's probably just a conventional notion spawned from adolescent heads.

But historically, venereal disease has spread with almost every explorer. Somehow, discovery of cultural difference and a sense of power and control get mixed together with sexual exploration and exploitation. Physical rape and cultural rape go hand in hand, driven by the unnamed quest to prove oneself. The greatest way of honoring and sharing love is demeaned and used to humiliate.

The returning servicemen I mentioned ate in the Bean Hall, and because the housing facilities were overtaxed, some were tucked here and there on the high school campus. Whiskey bottles were stored on windowsills. They smoked, swore, and did just about anything they wanted. Most came back to learn as well as to take advantage of the GI Bill, but many also seemed to come back to raise hell. We high schoolers watched the returning heroes from outside the loop. They had won the war, but they were not the white knights we still wanted to make them. So, many of them gradually fell from the pedestals we had put them on. I was ripe for disillusionment, and they helped me along.

It was understood at the school that the class officers were supposed to help make social life at the school fun, and I was junior class president. The guys spontaneously got dates with the particularly good-looking girls or the fast girls. But helping social life with the rest was a real arm twister. "Come on, I'm taking Sue; she's a dog. Surely you can take Sally." Talk about prejudice based on mere appearances! What those girls endured should never have happened. Our social job was also making sure that the girls got walked home. We didn't have to like it, and we usually didn't even pretend that we did. On one such occasion I found myself self-right-eously setting an example by walking home one of the leftovers.

I tried to make the best of it. The streetlight was behind us, and so I teased her by making shadows of our heads coming together as if we were necking. She seemed to know it was all air, and countered with talking about foot-ball. I played football at the time mostly because it was the thing to do and certainly did not live for the game. But she knew every player's number and position and even seemed to know most of the plays. I got the feeling that she knew every tackle I had missed. It seemed strange that she was so involved, since she was the daughter of the wealthiest family in town. I went home with one big impression. She knew too much about football for any girl.

During the school year I did odd jobs to make spending money. Occasional money came from home, but regular allowances were just not part of the program. My main employer was a cousin who had married into the same wealthy family. I was a sort of poor relative, and he was "helping me out." It made me mad, because my cousin was only nine years older than I was, and I knew where he had come from. He didn't seem to remember. I began a sort of love/hate relationship with money. I wanted to have enough but had a hard time respecting those who had too much.

My cousin had a black cook and also a black babysitter who came down from "the big house." Sometimes when she couldn't come, I babysat the kids. I was "help" sometimes, and yet I was also a cousin away from home. I would be invited to meals. It wasn't their intention, but I felt that while I had a place at their table, I also had my place. I began to learn how hard it is to take care of other people's kids. You have to love them or the kids won't respond. But if you're the one who changes them, tosses them in the air and kids them...One time in college I was left in charge of the kids for a couple of weeks while their parents were on vacation. The parents came home, and the father went to lift the two-year-old out of his high chair. The child's hands shot towards me, and he cried out, "No! Uncle Bob!" It was one of the few times I ever saw my cousin wilt. I loved the kids, but never wanted to undercut family bonds. I wilted too. I guess black domestic help has faced this dilemma since slavery. You feel your way to uncertain boundaries. But when the mother says, "He's so good with the kids," you crawl. Being "like one of the family" can split you in half. At this point, finding boundaries seemed to be the story of my life.

About that time I got a summer job in Chicago and had to commute every day by train from the little town where I was born. It was a clanging and sooty experience. But more than that, the backyards of the poor always seem to be next to the tracks. At a distance, with the soot jumping between the panes of the double-glazed window, I saw and I wondered...at a distance. I'd taken the train to town before, but seeing the garbage, the junk, the big and little filth every day, it began to sink in. Even walking from the station to the factory office, litter stuck to my shoes. I sure wouldn't want to live there. It never occurred to me that most of the inhabitants didn't want to live there either.

This was perhaps some sort of beginning of social consciousness, but it spoke more to a vague feeling of injustice than to reflective thought. Injustice could still be applied in comfortable general terms. The city's poor were simply that. Blacks were all blacks. I didn't even recognize the difference between Southern and Northern, between American and African, or African and African. It was far from a personal cause. Social issues were still non-issues for me. There are lots of us like that.

Ignorance doesn't excuse, but does it condemn? An ignorant person can learn. He can even learn to get involved. In contrast, a knowledgeable person with confirmed prejudice has to unlearn a lot of things before he can be a part of any solution. Fortunately, I was not accused of hatred and prejudice. I know that it hurts if people are seemingly unconcerned and uncaring as I was. But I had the opportunity to learn because no one at that time closed my mind by challenging and condemning my supposed motives. All whites are no more the same than all blacks are, and any real solution must begin with that clearly understood. Racial and cultural generalizations are usually the props of conventional prejudice.

The so-called "economic royalists" were pitted against the blue-collar union workers throughout most of my childhood. During the war both my mother and father had to join their respective unions in order to join the work force serving the war effort. They learned the overwhelming power of the union leadership. Many like them, partly from fear, did not attend the meetings. This allowed the leadership to claim to be responsive to the majority who attended, because the others had no voice or did not make it heard. Politicians are masters at wooing and manipulating any definable group, cultural, racial, or economic, but it is always at the expense of those outside. Unless the group rises above the conventional level of behavior, they are easy prey for manipulation. The easiest power base is a generalized group which puts its own needs above that of humanity.

Towards the end of senior year, I got a job offer from my cousin's father and mother-in-law. It involved "working" at their summer estate, being part of a social group of young people for each other and for their family and friends—available to hike, play tennis, and watch grandchildren swim, along with cutting grass and simple maintenance. I remembered the daughter. "She knew too much about football," and that didn't show promise. I was frankly uneasy about what looked like a summer outside of my element, sort of being there to play when needed. I decided that it wasn't for me.

Then my cousin got to me. "I was missing a unique experience." "He had had a wonderful time when he took a job there." I already was beginning to think that what was good for him, in his mind was good for everybody. But since I had no other job, and my best friend the Canadian had decided to go, I changed my mind and said yes. What the heck.

Our first job was helping pack for the trip. I remember the specially sized handmade wooden boxes for quantities of classical records. At that time records were extremely breakable and had to be packed just so, and a symphony like Beethoven's Ninth sometimes took as many as six records. By now I had been to a couple of youth concerts and even recognized the Tacotta and Fugue. But how could anybody go to so much trouble just to be able to choose what they wanted to listen to, even to having several different conductors' versions of the same piece? Packing the cars and getting ready, I met the two black house men. They were wonderful fun guys. In the workplace I was further down the totem pole than they. Still, my roommate and I ate with the family. They didn't. We went on all the social activities. They didn't.

At the summer place there was a Spanish-American whom we really liked and who became our immediate boss. Actually he was Catalan and wanted us to know. He had a tremendous admiration for Mr. & Mrs.. He was much more of a "friend" of the family than the house men, but he still had a place and kept it. His role was like ours: "help," but part of the family as to meals and social activity. His loyalty seemed almost like hero worship, but it was not blind and seemed to be freely given from a combination of admiration and conviction. Subtly, as we cut trails and views together, he opened my eyes to a view of that family and the trail they were walking. Religion was an integral part of almost everything they did, not self-consciously or self-righteously a part, but a pervading influence.

The family obviously had an affection for the regular servants. Teasing requires familiarity, and they teased Lena the cook about baseball. She played every game on the radio loudly to overcome kitchen bangs and rattles. Most of us cheerfully shared baseball and weather conversations as we walked through the kitchen. The Mrs. went much further. She knew the names of all their children and inquired about them. They also "discussed" religion and politics, but I felt the conversation was a bit one-sided. I wondered whether they felt pressured, just took an easy way, or were really interested.

The boss was a remarkable man. Trained as a lawyer, a tremendous lay student of religious doctrine, he not only saw the principles, he stuck to them. Right was right and wrong was wrong. Justice, discipline, and fairness seemed to be part of almost everything he ever did. I can still see him practicing his violin fingering on a violin stem without playing a note.

He was a broad student of Lincoln's life, and spoke frequently to our school. He admired the way Lincoln stood for fundamental principles and yet protected individual worth through those unifying principles. He saw Lincoln's human greatness in his respect for humanity from a Bible-centered conscience.

He also wrote a special pamphlet called "Americans All" for immigrants seeking citizenship. He had several times spoken at Lincoln University and supported the United Negro College Fund. He saw the racial issue as a political cause. Because it was also much more than political, it meant he should try to do something about it. But whatever he did had to be consistent with human freedom and dignity. He was clear that the Democratic government housing, welfare, and social programs violated human dignity and were not the way to go. Education and fair employment practices were. The company he headed had a motto, "Profit with honor." He put some thoughts behind my budding conservative politics and at the same time fleshed out some of my social concerns.

His life was structured, and part of that discipline was family worship every night. We sang hymns; he read from the Bible and the Doctrine; we prayed together. Family worship was something I had never experienced before. It was not emotional, but it had depth, warmth, and purpose. When he went away on business, we boys were asked to lead worship. It was awesome. It was the key to their family integrity, and we were trusted. In a strange sort of way, I think conducting worship for the family inspired my taking another look at the daughter. She stood for something deeper than had ever even mattered to me in a girl before.

The black servants were invited to worship. Though they had their own churches, since they were not able to attend them they were free to attend family worship in the evenings or family Church on Sunday. They were "free," but even then I wondered what sort of hidden pressures they felt. Were they free? They could not just walk away. I was sure they did not agree with everything, but I never heard them express it. I was of the same religion. I could discuss, and did. After all, I hoped to be a minister one day. I am sure the pressure was unrecognized and unintended, but I'm just as sure that it was there.

Mr. and Mrs. had a remarkable harmony of conviction and life. They had their principles of life right down into their house rules. Their rules were tight, but you knew the boundaries. He was the spokesman for order, but I came to know that she was often the staying power behind him. She was not physically strong, but in matters of conviction she was adamant. Considering the difference

in backgrounds they were tremendously
accessible to us. At meals Mr. would often
pull out a clipping from the *Wall Street
Journal* and open the discussion of current
events or politics. Religion too was a
common topic. If they stood apart from
others, it was on issues of religious
conviction, not the superficial differences of
supposed position. We believed as they did,
and that was the bond.

As a very small minority Church we have
struggled under clear but subtle burdens.
Even if talking about religion is often taboo,
society in general is highly tolerant of religion. From its broadminded heights, society
usually accepts the New Church. We have a
choice. We can accept their ecumenical tolerance, make ourselves as much like everyone
else as we can, and run the risk of being
swallowed. Or we can pull back, declare our
differences and be branded as an unreason-
able cult.

Like most minorities, we have tended to
choose to stress our differences and build
walls. More recently we have felt "strong"
enough to wrestle with societal pressures.
Being tolerated is perhaps one of a minority's
most dangerous roles if it wishes to maintain
its integrity. There is nothing to stand up to,
and that often means that you lose what you
stand up for. But when we yield to the
dominant culture, we often end up hating

ourselves for our weakness or for what we have lost. This potential loss of racial integrity will be, in fact is, a very real challenge for the blacks as tolerance and acceptance increase. It is a different level of individual against conventional values, i.e. individual groups against larger cultural and societal groupings.

At this point I was ready to stand up as an individual and be counted as different, in most things. Being different is more important than being accepted as we test our conventional boundaries. I had been raised a Republican, but had only thought of the issues in terms of being made fun of by Democratic schoolmates who were the majority. The Mr. organized local Eisenhower support. We all "liked" Ike. He had an almost childlike appeal to our sense of fairness and justice. I had almost no idea of the issues, but in a strange way idealized Ike. He was part of the pride of victory. Mr. P. got his daughter and her friends to go down to the factories and hand out campaign buttons. In his zeal, not realizing the harassment they were exposed to, he laid the plans and they complied. I was a bit concerned for her safety, felt protective, and had no idea why.

The blacks of the household also went to the rallies. They were asked, and they painted and carried placards. It was good to have blacks showing their support of the Republican cause. I have often wondered since just how real that support was. For all his dedication to freedom, Mr. P. never seemed to realize the influence and the power of his position. Perhaps, with his sense of principles and candor, he felt that his assertion of freedom was enough. If he said that they should feel free, that should mean that they felt free. Since he was so independent, they should be too.

The estate was on top of a mountain in the Catskills; actually it *was* the mountain. On one side the reservoirs of New York City's water supply sparkled in the wind, or reflected the clouds and mountain panorama in the calm. From the porch just off the living room you could watch the sunset behind a ridge broken by peaks. Ve, the daughter, and I used to sit on the porch and "interpret" the sunsets. The interpretations were really chances to share as yet undefined thoughts and feelings by a sort of innuendo. Reds could be opportunities to say what made you mad or what warmed you. But gradually the sunsets and interpretations faded, and we just talked.

Sometimes we played classical music in the background. The amplifier was especially sensitive, and Ve was allowed to change the records, but her father did not want anybody else to use it lest we get careless. Even long

playing records only went ten minutes or so.
It was maddening to have to break the sphere
by saying, "Record, Ve." So it was more usual
to watch the sunset without music and listen
to the music when we joined the others after
dark. To this day classical music is a background for reflection, not something that
requires full focus. One possible exception is
the Negro spiritual. They had some Marian
Anderson, Paul Robeson, and many others.
Their simple purity held us.

Ve's point of view was always interesting.
Somehow it was moving without being argumentative. I had never experienced close
friendship with a girl. It was a whole new
dimension. She saw things and felt things I
would never have seen or felt without her.
She inspired me to think and talk confidently about my own feelings and my goals,
then she influenced and bent them without
any appearance of pushing. She was a different friend than any I had ever known. I was
just beginning to appreciate what a girl
could be, or was it what this particular girl
could be to me?

I had seven more years of schooling before I
would be a minister, seven years before I
could really think seriously about supporting
a girl. Jobs make money. But they are much
more than that. By making us of service to
others they bring responsibility and self-
respect. Being useful is a key way for one to

find an individual place, but in collective society. Employment opportunities can in some measure be legislated. But a sense of being useful to others is acquired not through law but through the inner sense of belonging that responsibility to society generates.

This redeeming force of being useful is an enormous challenge in Third World countries. I remember well a visit from a young man as I sat in the luxury of my hotel in Ghana. He was little more than the age I had been during that summer in the mountains. He was trained in Tech School as an accountant. He had immigrated to the city, yet had no work. He was thin and drawn, obviously hungry when I offered him food. His clothes were not going to impress prospective employers if there were any. His youthful dreams of success had dried up under the hot sun of African economic reality. His pride broken, he stood as a symbol of so many, so many I could not possibly help beyond a few demeaning dollars as a handout. There simply must be a sufficiency of economic opportunity to allow an individual to find his useful place among his neighbors. Serving and being served allows us to belong.

In Ghana many, perhaps most, of the young men migrate from the simple villages to the big cities to seek work and—let's face it—excitement and adventure. It is their way to break free of the conventional strictures of village life. Looking for work, excitement, and adventure, are they so different from everybody else? But jobs are few. In the city, as in the villages, a few plots exist where you can gain primitive self-sufficiency if all else fails. But mostly the houses crowd in on both sides of the dusty streets. The gutters are full of slop. Some people beg. Some drift. Many will do almost anything to subsist. Idealism and pride erode. I've watched gangs of them, heads cocked, pushing and shoving each other, their rhythm and pace trying to somehow cajole each other to feel they can be someone.

In a young men's discussion one evening a young man said, "All the smart young people come to town." I thought a moment and asked, "Where is the best moral behavior, in the villages or here in the city?" "In the villages," they all replied. "Yet you say the smart ones come to the city?" I asked.

Will they go with the crowd to pursue an elusive dream, or will they take a stand as individuals for what they know is right? Can they truly be happy where they cannot use their God-given talents in the work place? Spiritual growth needs to be ultimated in day-to-day work and life. Being useful bonds us to our neighbors. They need jobs, even just plain ordinary jobs.

In that same discussion the Ghanaian young men cornered me on the question of

interracial marriage. I explained that I felt
where there were sincere hearts looking to
God together, a mixed racial couple could
overcome the external and social hardships.
Some grew sensitive. Perhaps I saw too many
hardships. The local pastor jumped in and
said, "Now wait a minute. Up until only a few
years ago no one from my tribe would ever
marry a person from yours." One of the tribes
had been allies of the British before
Ghanaian independence. So much of prejudice is a mindless group reflex. Wherever we
live, we have to do our own thinking in order
to appreciate those others who are beyond
the stereotypical conventions handed down
from one generation to the next. My Dad
served in the First World War, and I still have
to fight his prejudices and mocking of the
French, the "frogs."

It happened that on that same morning I
had talked with the Belgian about black
women being better. I reflected on the
prostitute in many cases selling her body to
wealthy tourists as the only way to provide
for those she loves. Perhaps as she
humiliates herself she tries to separate her
response and feelings from the bed of one she
truly loves at home. But what of the effect
upon the men sitting in that room discussing
racial issues with me? When a man cannot
provide and his wife stoops to prostitution,
how does the man feel? I know the real

answer is in higher values, but there is some truth in Maslow's scale.

It is not only Ghana; it's Chicago and New York. The difference is that in Accra more perhaps go home to try to live normal lives with husbands. But what does this pervading disillusionment do to the whole developmental process in the home? What did the southern slaveholder's sleeping with the slave girl do, not just to the girl but to her black husband? We cannot dismiss the need for change in economic circumstance, but we must realize that simply changing economics won't bring about a new covenant between races and cultures.

Denial is no answer. Yet it is there, over and over, in so many different circumstances. In terms of restoring human dignity, what is the answer to the street beggars in Ghana? Even the Ghanaians themselves tend to deny by saying, "Most of them are refugees from Chad."

In contrast, there is something special and admirable in the villages. Even if too often the fathers are in the city, the immediate family and the greater community family raise the children with bonding and idealism laying strong humanitarian and charitable foundations. But the young see just enough of another way of life that the more ambitious among them are not content with the conventions and simple physical jobs in the village. If economically and humanly rewarding work could be developed before disillusionment set in, they would have a basis for stability and growth. But tending cocoa trees or working at cottage crafts won't challenge many of these bright young minds. Education stirs ambitions which simply must be fed.

The greater community family was even more challenged in the townships of South Africa. The mythical idealism of the culture eroded. Gangs rebelled against tribal values and fashioned their own conventional rules. They defined themselves by being against "whitey" and all he stood for. And they responded with violence and aggression.

Civil law, as we have said, is the underpinning for conventional order and behavior. But that law must be just. Without just civil law, how can a young person find his way to a responsible individual place in society? He has no course but to try to repair society first.

During apartheid, one of my friends was offered a ride to the bus on a rainy night by his college professor who happened to be a white female. The police forced him out of the car into the pouring rain for alleged fraternization. In those times he was lucky. He could have been jailed. Should the too-frequent violent response surprise us?

In the tension between Inkatha and African National Congress, the mother of one of our minister's was shot in the leg while he dove out the window to escape. It goes on and on.

It's commonplace. Think of the sorting young blacks must learn to do if a New South Africa is truly to emerge.

In youth, many in this country also want to break out of the conventional box and rebel. The behavior of young people in the sixties was a good example. Individual reflection can open the way to a further development of faith. But if it does not lead us to care for others, it remains purely subjective and ultimately violates the early need for a sense of belonging. Without serving others and being served there is no stable or lasting relationship to society. At best it ends in situation ethics. At worst it only looks after "number one." Genuine society exists on the basis of interlacing usefulness. An individual conscience which is based on freedom and useful responsibility to others under God is the key to being accepted in the human family. But acquiring that conscience is a step which many do not and in some cases apparently cannot take.

Our church in South Africa has a new preschool. Very gradually our churches are integrating on Sunday morning. My grandchildren play with coloreds and blacks. But the basic sense of security has got to be upheld. Think of Washington D.C., Detroit, Chicago, Los Angeles. How can we help the young work their way through their anger and frustrations to a conscience which is based on trust, ideals, and stable standards of behavior? I often think of those psychological studies of remedial reading which reintroduced students to crawling and other movements which were missed in the early years. What do we reintroduce for those youths who have an undeveloped sense of trust and cultural idealism? How does an adult rebuild a sense of trust when he or she knew so little of it as a baby? What kind of emotional crawling is necessary to recoup even partially what has been lost? We all have such gaps, but we need to look closely at our development in order to learn what we are missing. We have thoughtful work to do, for it is not only the blacks who should be singing "We shall overcome."

VI

▼

COLLEGE PLUS
CRITICAL REFLECTION AND FAITH

When I returned for College, I immediately
enrolled in a religion and philosophy major.
Almost as immediately I entered a new and
exciting social pattern which included Ve as
often as possible. Her father would wait up for
her—playing the violin while I burned. Her
father and mother had rules, and they made
me mad, but I respected them. Underneath I
always knew they respected and even liked
me. After all, they had invited me to their
summer home and trusted me in a great
many ways.

Ve and I went to concerts, played bridge,
listened to music, went to parties, etc. But the

long walks through the scented fields and
woods were the real treasure. They were
shared sorting times as each of us tried to
find what the other really thought, hinting,
probing, watching. Here was someone whose
way of dealing with a thing was totally different from mine. I analyzed and ponderously
questioned; she went to the heart of it. We
both began to find out who we were in our
own right as we revealed ourselves and discovered one another. The shape of a cloud led
to shared hopes. A tiny wildflower drew out
thoughts of the Lord's beauty. The wonders of
light and shadow, trees and clouds, together
with our basic faith, which we both loved,
kept us focused. We discovered that special
trust which is at the heart of every genuinely
human relationship. No subject was off limits,
except expressing what we felt for each other.

We had been taught from childhood that
marriage was eternal. For years we had imagined our eternal partners and had even been
trained to pray that the Lord would provide
one special person with whom we could grow
forever. She seemed to fit the model: we were
growing so fast. She was not a princess, but
simply the closest friend I had ever known.
Really talking about our concerns and our
hopes could not help but reveal weaknesses.
Even then I had no doubt that she saw my
limitations, sometimes even more clearly than
I. But we were looking at potentials. Were they

merely multicolored dreams, passing sunsets, or could they become a reality?

Unconsciously and consciously we were applying to our relationship the tools we had acquired in the earlier stages of our faith. We were deeply moved by mutual trust. We shared peace and contentment. Like toddlers running and turning over new things, we explored our past experiences and shared new ones every time we met. We clarified our moral roots and confirmed mutual values. Every date I thought of "happily ever after." Justice, integrity, affection, beauty, and wonder blended into a set of ideals that we not only saw clearly, but were determined to foster. It was to be not just what others had taught us, but our set of rules of life. When she asked what I thought about some issue, *my* thoughts—not someone else's—had to make reply. Her feelings had to be hers now—not something from habit or tradition. Her probings were part of making my faith my own and—the wonder of it!—*our* own.

Both of us were the youngest in our families and knew the stress of the bottom-up family network. While we later strongly declared our independence from both families, at this point, because we appreciated each other so much, we each appreciated where the other one came from.

I had trouble appreciating my Dad, who seemed to make being friends with everyone, no matter what they were like, the most important thing in life. She got me to focus on how important and human that affection was. She had trouble with her father's always seeming to act coldly and rigidly on principles and rules. Through me she began to see how much he really cared, and that living his principles was his way of showing it. You could hardly find more different men than my father and her father, but somehow through each other's eyes we were discovering how to appreciate both of them for who they were. In many ways we knew what we were leaving, but were only just beginning to know where we were going.

From our upbringing we brought very different baggage to the table. Our social and economic backgrounds were almost at opposite poles. But I already loved our religion so much that I wanted to be trained as a minister to serve the institution of the Church. She loved our religion so much that she inspired me to want to serve the *people* of the Church. Male and female created He them.

In our own ways we each wanted desperately to be individuals. It was where we were in our lives. But in the wisdom of Providence we were learning to be individuals together. It was like two paths coming together and forming one going in the same direction but three times as wide. Isn't that the real challenge of handling human difference: to be ourselves, but together? We were both trying to sort through all the conventions we had been trained to. We knew there were many we couldn't accept—but we pushed off together and loved it.

Our faith had a long way to go. Indeed, if faith cannot be perfected to eternity, our path of constant growth and renewal together was the wrong path. In a strange way I think that the way that I proposed and that she responded tells where we were. We were on a long spring walk savoring the smell and crunch of our favorite pinewoods. Sensing nature's wonder together, thinking together, feeling together. As we sat under the deep green of the trees doodling with the pine needles, I saw my best friend with his then best girl across the valley. I had long looked at all the reasons why and why not to propose. I knew that I wanted to, but did not know how or even when. As we both looked at the couple across the way I said, "Do you think that couple will last?" I think she picked up something from my voice or perhaps read something else, and she looked not at me, but questioningly into me. I then asked, "Do you think we will last?" She looked a little uncertain, then I added, "I mean forever." She relaxed and said smiling, "I don't see why not." I kidded her for years that she didn't say "Yes," but only "I don't see why not."

As I have looked at my own children at that same age, or at students in my classroom, or at the young people who come to me as pastor and earnestly ask, "How do you know if you are in love?" I think how immature they all are. And I gratefully marvel that somehow the Lord led me to the wisest decision of my life when I myself was so naive, even stupid.

The day after I proposed we were scheduled to go to a Philadelphia Orchestra concert. Ve's aunt was to chaperone, and the chauffeur would ease the Cadillac around to pick up the crowd that evening. Of course after I had proposed, Ve went home to tell her mother, and instead of going to the concert I had the big appointment with her parents. Ve was sent to the concert. She had explained to her aunt that I couldn't come because I wasn't feeling well. Unfortunately, they drove by as I walked up to the house to see my future "Mama and Daddy." Seeing me, the old aunt simply said, "You're right, Bob doesn't look very well."

Their house had a tower with a wonderful view. Ve and I had spent many evenings looking out on Philadelphia's lights to the south and the stars to the north. If we were lucky we watched the sliver of a new moon, our favorite kind, which always seemed to speak to the promises of the future. I was to meet with her parents in the privacy of the tower. It was not the same place that night.

Her father started off forthrightly enough, "I certainly hope that you two young people do not think that you are engaged." I replied, "I don't know exactly what else you would call it." At that point Ve's mother burst into tears. Not one of my best moments. Somehow we managed to get through the meeting with some mutual respect, but we did not announce our engagement for some time. There was no doubt in *our* minds even if it wasn't "official."

I see now that the real problem was that we were young and that they felt that I should be in my job, and I still had five years of schooling ahead of me. Ve and I of course knew better. I was already part-time employed and we, at least, were sure that with care in a few years we could swing it, even without her inheritance. Those extra hours of part-time work were important to me, as I had to be convinced that money was not influencing my love for Ve. Still, in the back of our heads we both knew that nothing I earned as a minister would ever make much difference to the support of our family.

If you ever want to learn that money is not the measure of a man, marry sincerely into it. You will learn that you have it even if you don't work. You have to know that you are willing to work hard, not because your work is needed to support your family but for the sake of being useful to others. When society measures your usefulness and pays you accordingly, it implies a conventional form of being valued. Money as a measure of human worth is one of the leading elements that holds back faith development in this country. If you as an individual work to serve society because you know you should, you as an individual are reaching for your own measure of usefulness. Being useful to others and having a sense of belonging and being accepted go hand in hand. We were focused on my future use, but still packing for the journey.

In our differences we discovered our need for each other. To be useful to others I needed her inspiration and point of view, even as she needed mine. Without the other, each of us was only half a use. Human difference and the need for others go hand in hand. National, racial, and cultural differences are part of what creates a need for each other, just as male and female are. But the God-given and cultivated talents in each one of us reach closer to the heart of day-to-day needs and the appropriate response to them. You need many talents to build a skyscraper or even a tiny computer chip. You need countless thoughts and affections to shape the mind of a child.

Dignified employment both in the home and outside it in society is vital to expressing our humanity to others. It is not what the job pays, but who, what, and how it serves that measures a man. In this country, if when we think of the need for opportunity equal pay becomes our measure, the growth of what is truly human will be stunted. Pay may reflect some measure of usefulness, but usefulness in and of itself is the real measure of the man.

Poverty is dreadful and debilitating. But we must not set our sights only on providing enough to live on. Give every citizen the ability to both cultivate and use his talents to the full for the sake of others, and you will give him his dignity. Give him gratitude and appreciation for his service, and you give him happiness and acceptance.

I feel very grateful that I attended a religious college. I was even more grateful that Ve and I had a few classes together. Many secular universities do an outstanding job of challenging traditional and conventional values—a challenge so necessary for the development of faith. But as they prod the student to declare his independence from convention, many universities tend to leave him in a vacuum as to values. They take the student to the point of existential self-assertion, but often fail to provide the tools for truly human self-realization. It is one thing to think critically about what our values should be as we seek our place in society. It is quite another to arrogantly demand proof of humanity's spiritual foundations. Humanity demands a covenant of absolutes, but freedom demands that there be no compelling proof of that covenant. Can we not come to acknowledge an all-wise God who reveals Himself in such a way as to preserve our freedom, and with it our ability to love?

In a literature class we were studying *Walden*. Thoreau's withdrawal seemed to me like a cop-out from responsibility. The importance of being useful was really big for me just then. I couldn't see what the price of potatoes had to do with life and said so in mocking terms in class. After putting up with me for a sufficient time, the teacher simply said, "Jungé, if you are going to be so darned cavalier, you can get out of class." Ve said later that as my neck turned red she felt she could hear me breathing, but I settled down. In my search for values I could challenge Thoreau, but I could not be arrogant. Arrogance is the danger in the assertion of radical individualism. Arrogance and conceit will destroy any potential for a genuine human relationship with our fellow men.

Academia is dedicated to the process of inquiry. But all too often in their zeal to make their own contribution to their fields, academics spar with each other like lawyers in the courtroom. They become so careful and defensive of their case that, despite their words to the contrary, they only want their own thoughts parroted back to them. In their efforts to make good grades, students can easily then fall into the pattern of a kind of literalism using learned articles or quotations to confirm positions and theories. Students are distracted from independent thought and the free choices it defines. Religious institutions are particularly vulnerable to this stifling form of teaching. In effect they impose a conventional faith upon their students. The religious institutions of the world themselves need to learn to cope with diversity, even perhaps to celebrate it as coming from the wisdom of our Creator. Is it not possible to come to believe wholeheartedly in your religious convictions, and yet grant that in the wisdom of God someone else's belief system may be best for them?

Learning is not an end in itself. A friend of mine, the son of one of my teachers, one evening in a beer session uttered some profound and erudite thoughts on relativity. His father stepped from the next room and said, "Yes son, and there are a lot of people who say two plus two doesn't equal four, and nobody gives a damn about that either." He was a philosophy and theology professor. He cared about Einstein, but he cared about life more.

One of my teachers who had come into our Church as an adult and was a strong supporter of Church outreach was our advisor for a college discussion group. I presented an impassioned plea for advertising the church, for public lectures, and for all the forms of modern communication. I had called radio stations and newspapers to put a price tag on the proposed program. Much of the discussion was stridently critical of our Church's alleged isolation. The group enthusiastically urged a dynamic and dramatic change to persuade others to join our cause. Our advisor got up at the end and simply said, "I don't know much about spreading the Church, but I do know a little about fishing, and I know that the ones who catch the most fish don't make the most noise."

Putting his comment in perspective with Ve the next night, my balloon was still popped. But I came to see that programs were not the primary way to serve my lifelong vision of sharing the Church with others. Being human and caring is the life of any program. Freedom, not persuasion, is at the core of all genuinely religious growth.

Sparring and quoting, analyzing and arguing to see the implications of the doctrine are part of a theological student's daily diet. The integrity of the Doctrine drawn from the Word of God is the foundation. We can never come out of ourselves and humbly focus on others unless we acknowledge a set of God-given principles which tell us what good is, even if they run counter to what we think we want. Conventional and traditional faith can control behavior, but cannot change the heart. Our

faith will not grow simply by rejecting convention; it must be infilled and enhanced so that
it lets God talk to our individual conscience
and form our unique loves.

Under Ve's tutelage, the more nits and nats
of theology I studied, the more I felt that it
was religion that was needed. The more sermons I wrote like legal briefs, the more she
tried to turn me into an advocate in the decisions in the courtroom of life. I still remember
one comment she wrote in the margin of one
of my sermons, "Only my mother and the
Bishop are still listening."

It was not all altruistic. When I went home
for the summer, I knew that Ve's family kept
horses. So I invested in riding lessons, which
I never mentioned in my long letters. I duti-
fully walked that darn beast with its nose up
the rear of the next horse in front, week after
week. It was going to be such a special surprise in the fall. When I told Ve in the fall, it
turned out that she loved horses, but was
afraid to ride them and heartily disliked it. We
were learning, big things and little.

She took a part-time cooking course to, in
the proverbial manner, be "able to cook like
my Mom." Her family's cook had ruled the
kitchen, and there was no place for the
daughter of the house to learn. In the course
Ve learned to cook very well, well enough to
cook and entertain thirty or forty at special
dinners, but it was never her real interest or

love. Part of it was that I had cooked since I was a kid. If I could do it, there wasn't the same kind of need, or perhaps appreciation.

But when it came to fixing up the little house we would live in when we got married, she was in her element. She rose to the challenge of making curtains for every window. The colors and patterns needed to blend perfectly with the walls I was painting. It was then that I began to think of women as "sphere builders." She was so concerned about the "feel" of a room. I just wanted to get done.

Ve is a perfectionist. I'm more willing to do things quickly—but I too hold pretty high standards for myself and particularly for others. My mother-in-law saw this as a challenge for each of us in being too critical. Neither of us felt we were better than others, since our critiques applied to us as well as them. Still, the standards we use in evaluating others tend to define our relationship to them. If our standards are not generally accepted, we will be set apart as a minority. Our difference will often be perceived as, "You think you're so much better." And to preserve our integrity, it is easy to become defensive and withdraw, which doesn't make it any better. Couples just setting out are often so content with each other that they spend a great deal of time alone—implicitly and often explicitly preferring their own company to society's. It's a neat providential arrangement that we learn to focus on one other before we take on the whole bunch. As different cultures labor to preserve and perfect their integrity, it is so easy to raise questions of which is better. Each new discovery can lead to withdrawal— "So there!" Finding our unique heritage can assert differences or it can lead to confident reaching out to and acceptance of others. It takes a lifetime to replace "I'm right," with "This is right."

We waited for just over three years to get married. It was not always easy. During that time I worked part-time and summer jobs. One summer job was being a handyman for a family at their summer home. They had hired a college girl to help look after the kids and cook. Unfortunately, the mother got sick and the college girl and I had a load of family cares thrown upon us. Ve's antenna went up. The more I tried to be good with the kids and learn about their care, the more she worried about my possibly getting too involved with the college girl. One evening Ve and I were lying on a big flat rock looking at the sky and she confronted me with her fears. What ambivalence for me! I wanted to respect her perception. Most men who are honest know that they have some tendency to at least look across fences. I could truthfully deny any real attraction, but not that there was some here and there thought. She was right, but she was wrong, and I was in the middle. Long silences and fitful conversation gradually yielded to open trust. Mutual confidence, common vision, and shared integrity meant that, given time, I loved her for her concern. The stars came out from behind the clouds.

Eventually the date was set. When Ve's father took us to New York to shop for her trousseau, I realized we were in for a grander wedding than I had imagined. In fact our experience in "Bird Dogs," as he called Bergdorf Goodman's, made me wonder if I would ever catch up or catch on. The little French restaurant he knew down some little side street wasn't any more convincing. I think, though, shopping with us was a turning point in his acceptance. I'm not sure that Ve's Mama really accepted us until she held our first child in her arms.

The preparations gradually maximized even to the hiring of a New York lighting expert for the church. When we objected to the brightness of the lights, he gestured with both hands and vehemently asserted, "If you want to be seen, you've got to be lit!" We weren't quite sure we wanted to be seen that much.

When I think about who I was—even who I still am, I wonder at Ve's courage in marrying me. I wonder at the courage of all women who marry. Here is a commitment at least for this life and hopefully forever to work together with another human being who approaches life quite differently. Yet because of the force of love, the heart is willing. Trust has been won and ideals shared and there is no turning back. Could God, through our marriages, teach us something very special in handling human differences of all kinds? Surely it is He who provides the love and trust which somehow give us the courage to go forward again and again with what we know is right.

When you walk up the aisle it all comes together—your love and trust for each other and God; your ideal castles which are way up there, but powerful forces for generating dreams; your little habits and mannerisms, those things you've been trained to which still unconsciously come into play and which you know so well in each other; the conviction of your reason that this is right, the confidence that now you will be on your own and make a home together. Marriage brings you to the peak of your capacity for faith development at the time. But since few can then be said to have a mature conscience, it seems that a wise Providence has planned the development of conscience as a mutual challenge.

I remember Ve's "going away" dress, with its little matching hat framing her face. Little white daisies danced on a yellow cotton background—so sunny and spring-like. I felt her innocence—almost as if she were a little girl. I was so determined to never hurt her. Our spring had come. There would be other seasons, even winters. But now it was spring, budding and beautiful in all its glory.

Will the races ever discover such a spring?

VII

▼

BEGINNING TOGETHER
COGNITIVE FAITH

During courtship we talked through a tremendous number of issues, but now we actually began to live through them. Our ideals confronted reality. When I was young and single, I asked God to help me. Now every day we asked Him to help us. Ve madc a special place for the Word on the bedside table. It was her "tradition," and it was a matter largely of her habits of conscience which drew us back whenever we forgot to read the Bible throughout our lives. I know of one minister who counseled couples, "Never go to sleep at night until you can say the Lord's prayer and kiss your spouse good night." A Mennonite friend says, "Be sure to pray together out loud; it is hard to stay mad at someone you hear praying to God out loud." Such tools were intrinsic "givens" to Ve, conventional norms which she made her own. Before I was married, everything seemed to be making up my mind, now it was our minds. It really is a wonderful and easy transition when you are in love. When the marriages in our society learn to pray, "Help us," we will be looking to God's first answer to radical individualism.

Where there is love there is freedom to be yourself, but there is no place for being radically alone. Self-realization enters a covenant—a coming together with another faithful and true self. True marriage is the profoundest honoring of human difference, and yet the Lord makes it easy through love. As you bring the unique treasures of your masculinity and femininity to each other and they are honored, you do not lose individuality. You gain it. You become more a man; she, more a woman.

Our honeymoon was three weeks in Jackson Hole, Wyoming. I can still smell the smoke of the pot belly stove that I lit in the cabin early in the morning while Ve slept in and watched at the same time. Some of the sunrise slides I took have halos from the frost on the lens when I took the camera from the warm car. During the day we lay in the sun watching the evergreens sway, letting the breezes stir deeper and deeper feelings to share. We were now united even as to bodies, and there was a new force in our lives. The streams bubbled and joined one another, as happy as we were. We climbed long mountain trails struggling higher and higher to express ourselves and discovering vistas we never imagined could exist. Praying to be us, completely.

After the honeymoon we returned to summer work and the little house we had so carefully groomed. It was brand new to feel her closeness in the next room while I struggled to get ideas through the typewriter and on to paper. She was within the process. I was there too, as she struggled with the mystique of pots and pans in the kitchen. Soon she was sick every morning as we looked forward to yet another wonder.

Both of our families presumed family bonds of which we were uncertain. T.S. Eliot speaks of a tendency away from rather than towards something definite. Though I had a pretty clear career goal, we felt that we had to somehow push off from our families. My father always wanted us kids to get together, but we didn't quite know what to do or say when we did. After we had admired each others' kids, what next? Ve's family was steeped in tradition. To me, at the time, none of her brothers and sisters seemed able to break out on their own. Everyone got together on Christmas, yet both Ve and I wanted to blend our Christmas traditions and start our own. At that time I think her folks had about forty grandchildren. All the babies and toddlers were in the living room in eight or ten playpens. It looked a bit like the Chicago stockyards. The same big table of fifty or sixty. The same menu. The same routine. We wanted something of our own, even though we couldn't fully identify it. Fortunately, we each felt the need for our "something" in contrast to our own family as well as in contrast to the other's. Perhaps we were precursors to the sixties generation and just didn't know it.

Our families were so different that if we were to really come together as a couple we had to shed many of those external differences and be ourselves. We were ready, though I'm not sure either of our families ever really understood.

Marrying a very wealthy girl who could easily support us if I never earned a dime was its own unique challenge. I had to be useful to others not just to provide things, but in order to win Ve's respect. Each day it became more and more important to be someone in her eyes and in my own. It was particularly hard to try to understand the vagaries of stocks and bonds when I was trying so hard to make being a student and part-time worker really important. In subtle ways, which I see mostly in retrospect, Ve alternately prodded and pulled back as I struggled to find out who I was. And then, wonder of wonders, she inspired me to try to focus on who I should be. The whole purpose of our uniqueness was that whatever we did, it was to be together.

It is fascinating that in the normal course of things the Lord sends children to give us the challenge of reaching beyond just each other. Personally, I think those who wait to have children miss the early opportunity for the Lord to show them in a natural and free way a whole new perspective on human needs. Our love for our children, if genuine, must respect their budding individuality, and yet we serve them with all our hearts. It began in that little house where in anticipation with paint brush and needle we prepared a tiny bed. God gave us a son. We had him in the same bed where he had been conceived. Everything was new. Being a mother was not just an addendum to Ve's life. It became new and wonderfully integrated into her personality. It was her. It was her life. If you think in terms of tenderly nurturing the spirit, there is scarcely any human responsibility more profound than motherhood. Our love for each other had a fresh way to express itself together in our love for the kids. But somehow I felt that my love for them came from and was sustained by hers. The Lord was gently leading us to think and work beyond ourselves, leading us outside of ourselves. A stable marriage and family leads our spirits one step at a time to accept others with love. The home energizes the roots for acceptance of others as they are and as the Lord would have them become. The truth is that the more we work together with our partners, the freer we become. That closeness brings untold mutual happiness.

When the home falters or breaks, the dynamics for working through prejudice in society stumbles as well. The God-given basic unit for teaching us to accommodate to others is being abandoned. Magnanimous "no fault" separations may sound very pretty as a rationalized acceptance of human difference. Many times in counseling, people proclaim that they want to give their partners freedom. But the argument is specious. In reality they are breaking the covenant they made to work through differences to a mutual and cooperative life with a fellow human being. The break-up of marriage pays tribute to irresponsible independence. The toll is the undermining of the foundation of society itself. What is more, the children's normal pattern of development is disrupted. Their sense of trust, of heroic idealism, of conventional order, of responsibility towards others, and of respect for religious covenants are all severely challenged when the home and family is severed. I question whether a society where divided homes are commonplace can ever effectively learn to handle human differences and prejudices. The normal God-given pattern for growth is aborted.

The Bishop's wife loved to tease. Just prior to my ordination she came up to Ve and said, "I know where you're going." And after a pause to try to arouse curiosity, "You're going to the mission in South Africa." Ve, quite sincerely, said, "Wonderful, Bob and I have often talked of it." At that point we'd have gone anywhere and taken any challenge. Our eyes were on the stars.

We actually went to Denver. Our back porch had a gorgeous view of the snow and crags of the Rockies. I can still see the blunted brown and white tip of Long's Peak looking back at us from behind the brown and green of the front range. It was so different from the familiar and comfortable mountains of the East. It was almost symbolic, reaching so high but so difficult to conquer. My assignment was to take a group of fifteen or twenty adult members and make it grow to be a full self-supporting congregation of perhaps fifty or a hundred. And, by the way, I was to travel all over from Seattle to New Orleans visiting members who had no pastor. I was away from home about 25% of my time. I could not really focus on the local people, nor on the ones I visited. After a year or two I realized I had an impossible job description, and set out to convince the Bishop that it was so.

The real blessing was that when I was home, I was home. My study was in our house. Since the local members were all ten or more years older than we were, we had almost no church social demands. So we had more time for each other and the kids than at any other time in my career. Whether it was where we were in life, my assignment, or whether it was selfish, we focused on each other, and we loved it.

Ve loved drawing and painting. Though she had had some private lessons, our marriage derailed her long-term desire to go to art school. I knew she would never go to night school alone downtown. So one evening a few months after the second of our seven children was born, I surprised her. "I've enrolled us in an evening water color class," I said. "I can't, I'm nursing a baby." "I picked one that comes between nursings, and Mrs. S. will come babysit."

We enrolled in many art courses after that, and she loved it. She is much more talented than I, but I basked in her enjoyment and learned to appreciate much more both her and art. In a natural, easy, and thoroughly enjoyable way I was helping her to be different and to become herself.

Most of what we consciously did for each other at that time was a positive effort to be nice and do what the other would like. This is part of accommodating to difference—but really only a beginning.

Similarly, races and cultures can do a lot for each other. They can learn about each other and try to be a part of the other's lives and interests. But positive action and appreciation are only part of an answer.

It is more difficult to break those habits and stop doing those little things which are a hair shirt to your partner. She tried to get ready on time. I tried to stay awake and listen when we went to bed. For a long time getting along took work, but it was relatively easy because it was mostly the outside of the cup and the platter and there were so many counterbalancing happy things.

We used to hold "meetings" in the car while the children played in the yard. There was privacy, and we discussed what we should work on with each child. Sometimes it meant suggesting that I not yell so much or face less obvious challenges. But we helped and accepted each other.

External acceptance and politeness, working to "get along" will also help smooth racial and cultural differences. Politeness paves the way, thoughtful, focused accommodation helps, but it is still only a partial answer. The subterranean streams of prejudice run very deep, fed by a seemingly limitless spring of selfishness.

With new babies coming along, we decided to get domestic help a couple of days a week. Ve had grown up with regular live-in domestic help. Her mother had weak health and read to Ve and played with her, but almost all the day-to-day care was given by a nanny. Cleaning, cooking, chauffeuring, etc. were all done by servants. We were not looking for that. We loved the integrity of our growing family too much for surrogates.

So came the advent of Petra, our first help. She was a tiny black-haired and fiery Spanish-American. Ve brought a very real affection for servants and a concern and care for them. She had an almost instantaneous rapport with them even though they came only once a week. Within a few days she chatted with Petra and knew what went on in her family.

Interestingly, at that time in Denver the Spanish-Americans were lower on the social scale than the blacks. It always "wonders" me how easy we find it to look down on those less fortunate than ourselves. Attitudes like these that are seemingly second nature make me look primarily for deeper human solutions rather than programs. Petra certainly felt put-upon by the blacks.

As Petra and Ve worked, they chatted all sorts of woman talk. I would sometimes stop and listen from my basement study and smile. I could never chat like that—seeming trivia clothing some really precious affections. I suppose men's talk of sports, politics, and religion, while very different, reads somewhat the same way to a woman. One day when Ve was going to my first funeral service, she asked Petra what she should wear. Petra replied, "When my husband died I wore a red dress." When Ve expressed surprise that Petra, a Catholic, didn't wear black, Petra said, "Oh, he was a bad man. Red was just the right thing." Symbols mean so much to women. They are an integral part of building atmospheres to which we men respond but hardly notice. It comes in their lifelong efforts to look nice. Every detail in the nest must "sing." Their handwork shows it. Gardens and plants testify to it. But you have to look within the symbol to begin to understand. Some say women are analogical while men are analytical. It's an enormously rewarding challenge to appreciate what makes the other tick. One and one make far more than two.

When Petra returned to Mexico, we got our first black help. Despite Ve's talent for getting close to the help, the interaction with daytime help is very different. They do their jobs and leave—and are not extensions of the family, as in the past or as it had been in Ve's home. Still, I began to use the opportunity to try to discover how they felt about racial issues. I was curious and always enjoyed the conversations and learned a lot. But I was never completely sure whether they welcomed the opportunity to talk or felt trapped. Maybe both.

I had one dramatic experience as a result of such discussions. Our black maid, Stacey, invited us to a banquet at her Church. Unfortunately Ve was sick and so I went alone. It happened that there had just been a serious racial incident in the South and all the black clergy had a hastily called meeting that night. After the meal, Stacey got up and said, "We have a very special guest here tonight." Being the only white in a room of a couple hundred, I had little trouble figuring out who the guest was. Then without warning she went on, "One time Reverend Jungé said that he thought the American Negro would be the means of bringing new life into the dead ashes of Christianity. I wonder if he will address us on that subject."

She was referring to a quotation from Toynbee, the historian, which I had shared with her. So I got up and spoke. I guess my theme was largely how we acquire prejudice, in fact are trained to it, and that they also must be very careful not to train their children to expect it. I just sort of rambled and said what I thought. Stacey thought it was great. I got quite a few "Amens," and "You said it brothers." I suspect that the response was good because I tried to be completely open.

Cultivating openness with those who are of the same background is not easy, but it is even more difficult with different cultures. Yet openness not only establishes your integrity as a person, but it honors and respects theirs. Trying to be politically correct and say the right thing is artificial and is perceived as artificial. The only thoughts and feelings which people should be careful about expressing are those which are reserved for sharing with spouses or intimate friends, or those they are ashamed of and are determined should be removed from their lives.

Domestic help often provides a limited and unbalanced view of race relationships. Many families in the circumstances we found ourselves in go through a long series of domestic employees. Listen to them swap stories about help over bridge or cocktails. Possibly the turnover is due to the job's seeming demeaning. Considering what I've heard said over those cocktails, that's not too surprising. One of our help always used to dress as if she were a secretary, putting on high heels, stockings and a fancy dress before she would run to the train home. Two women under the same roof may be another reason why the job often doesn't work out. We try to identify with them. We perhaps really want to understand, but there's often a strange unintended condescension involved. "If you had to scrub floors every day, wouldn't you...." Most of us are far less proficient at empathy than we realize. We lack the communication tools to let those working in our homes speak for themselves, so we imagine and guess.

I saw a wonderful example of this much later in life when I was going to Villanova University for an advanced degree. I had found the only black person in the seminar to be the most intelligent and interesting of the students. We had had many very open discussions between classes. The professor espoused all manner of economic, social, and political reforms. In trying to get discussion going she drew me out, which never was too hard. I said, "I do not feel that the problem needs money thrown at it. The programs are often sponsored by white political or social do-gooders, which makes the sponsors feel good and righteous but are essentially demeaning to the recipients." The professor, thinking that she now had a good discussion in the making, turned to the black student and said, "Now how do you feel about that?" He simply replied, "Sounds pretty good to me." In the next class she again got up on her stump and with emotional zeal harangued us about the dreadful conditions in the cities. Finally my black friend, who worked every day with young people in the inner city, had all that he could take. He did in that graduate seminar what only he could do. He began rhythmically clapping his hands and shouting, "Come on Mama, preach it to us. Come on, baby, preach it." I never saw a better put-down.

All of us, including myself, have to be very careful not to feel that we know the needs, let alone the solutions, when we have never walked in those moccasins. Many travelers see cultures through a video camera lens while hopping from capital city to capital city. I have always been fortunate and stayed largely with people native to the country in their own homes. But I was still a visitor and need to remember it. We can so easily make foolish generalizations, particularly when we have limited experience with a culture. Blacks of northern or southern origin are different. American blacks respond quite differently from African. Each African tribe has its own character. Yet many of us say, "Blacks feel this, blacks think that." It cuts both ways. I feel that I have been looked down on as a white because I'm presumed to be colonialistic, out for exploitation, etc. And I have had attributed to me, simply because I am white, feelings or motives that I either honestly don't have, or which I am sincerely fighting to control.

*   *   *

After seven years as a pastor, I was called to be Secretary of the international Church.

Neither Ve nor I really wanted to go, but I felt I was needed, and we went back to Ve's home town.

We had kept a file called "Dream House," and now had the opportunity to build it. It was early Pennsylvania architecture, about 1740, and we had an historical architect to design it. But Ve was involved in every detail. Every molding had to be perfect. She herself made scale drawings of the hardware. I really admired the painter's patience as he mixed one batch after another to get a color right. The house "sang." People loved its warmth and beauty. I loved my girl who did it.

A couple of years after we moved in, we turned our back on the offers of a property at the family complex in the Catskills and built the shell of a vacation home on a nearby Pennsylvania farm. Details were important, but during the summers the older boys, their friends, and I did much of the finished paneling and built and hung the doors on wooden hinges we made ourselves. The shell gradually got fleshed out. When you do the work yourself, you feel a delight and ownership which is very special.

But the farm had its moments for Ve and me. As a working farm, it had a manager who appealed to me for practical building and operational decisions. Inevitably, this led to questions of views and aesthetics, which meant so much to Ve. We had our children and their friends up for the summers. I worked hard on the house and farm with the boys. When we came in dog-tired at seven or eight in the evening from storing hay, Ve saw the opportunity for human relations and social life evaporate. Frequently the meals the girls had so carefully prepared were delayed and "ruined." We worked things out by bouncing from one tense decision or day to the next. Two different affectional needs were in conflict, but we worked it out because we both really wanted to and were beginning to focus more on those teenagers' needs than on our own concerns and needs.

There are many times when racial and cultural conflicts too feed upon different affectional needs. Only love for our neighbor can inspire a sustained desire to work it out. Good will or conscience can work wonders. But peace just won't happen without it.

The farm snuggled in the Pennsylvania hills on the edge of the Dutch country. Its softness touched tenderness in our hearts. But the community itself was aloof. We were newcomers and did not understand their paths. With our small town, minority-church mentality we enjoyed being left alone, and yet smarted a little and wanted acceptance. With their country neighborhood background, supported by its own language and culture, they didn't know whether they really wanted to accept us or wanted to excuse their reluctance by whispering that we were "offish." Two very traditional minorities were geographical neighbors. We could not share religion, language, and many cultural trappings, but after some twenty years we know friendship and trust. Not through pushing. Not without mistakes, but through patience and good will.

Having a farm manager and his family of "Dutch" background built a bridge here and there, because in our hearts we all wanted it. He and his wife wanted it. We wanted it. And the neighbors wanted it. When a neighbor had sickness or a barn burned, we were there. When we had trouble, their hands reached out. It has taken time—lots of time— but we have found a way to hold fast to our unique integrity and to respect theirs, yet still uncover and discover our common humanity. I really felt "in" when, at a cattle sale, the owner with seeming pride introduced a woman he was living with, but not as husband and wife. The Dutchman sitting next to me dug me in the ribs and said, "Vat vill ve cum to next?"

Marriages take time too. We make mistakes. We hurt each other. But with good will and patience, love and understanding, we become more masculine and more feminine. In that we are more uniquely ourselves, yet we are together.

There are times when marriage is like a reluctant hearthfire. The embers still glow, but it takes feeding, huffing, and poking to bring them to joyous flame again. Suddenly the warmth spreads and the colors shimmer with variety and promise again. The shadows here and there make contrasts to enhance countless imaginary dreams leaping, leaping upwards. We peek into another world as yet beyond our grasp, but so real. The hardwoods take longer to catch fire, but they last longer. The logs must keep close to sustain the flame.

One spring we took a fateful trip to Greece. We both loved the Greeks, the wonder of the Acropolis, Delphi, Patmos and so much more. The Greek children presented flower bouquets from sheer warmth, seeking no reward but our smiles and happiness. We imagined the character and feelings of those who worshiped behind the stately columns. It was then that I plaited a victor's crown of leaves and ceremoniously presented it to the little French boy visiting an ancient arena.

Ve and I loved thinking of those people 2500 years ago living a new vision of democracy. The vacation even gave us the added thrill of getting off the ship and being greeted by rifles and tanks in one of Greece's bloodless coups. When we called the Consul, he told us just to go about our business—but not talk politics. Of course Ve asked everyone we met about what was going on.

It was a wonderful, exciting, stimulating vacation. When we got back to the farm, however, I wanted to relax and digest what we had heard and seen. I felt so much at home I said, "This is even better than Greece." That was my first mistake, but I was even dumber than that. We began to compare our summer home which I had worked so hard on to our regular home which she had so lovingly designed. The discussion led to my saying that the only problem I had with our beautiful regular home was that it was so perfect I couldn't work on it or repair it. We pushed the hurt buttons as only those who know each other can. Yes, we got over it. I still remember it, and she has a much better memory than mine. Are the memories scars or construction materials? I suspect a bit of both.

As the races get to know each other well enough, they will push hurt buttons consciously or unconsciously. Courage and conscience will be the only answer.

Ve loved studying ancient art and cultures, particularly Egypt. She even read some hieroglyphics and talked me into learning some. She was fascinated with the early religions and loved comparing them to our doctrines. She particularly loved the ancient symbolism and the power it had for those peoples. She saw many lessons for our Church in this history and loved to talk about them. I felt that her "hobby" was beginning to take away from attention to the kids. I was not sure it was really "balanced and appropriate." But now I was clumsily challenging some of the things she particularly loved about her religion. Symbols helped her convey affection. What I said hurt terribly. I can still see the combination of fire and tears in her eyes as she said, "If you try to stand between me and the Lord and His Word, you just aren't going to do it." I came down off my high horse, and she backed off somewhat. I think we both realized that a sacred space exists between individuals and the Lord and belongs only to them. I hope I have learned to respect it.

Then too, each culture has its religious roots, its space if you please, between it and its Maker. Whatever a race or culture regards as its highest Good defines that space. When you get to know another culture well enough to know what it values most, then you are in a position to do enormous damage. Threats from other cultures to those spiritual treasures are the most devastating of all. The highest freedom is our freedom of religion. But freedom and love go hand in hand. And because we love our religion so dearly, it is very hard to foster others' freedom to love theirs. It is one thing to put its defense in our nation's constitution. It is quite another to protect our neighbor's freedom of religion from ourselves—to protect it not just from overt actions, but to respect it from our hearts without any subtle looking down.

Real communication involves a covenant— a free coming together, warts and all. Covenants involve common terms. For example, the whites in South Africa call for patience. It seems obvious to them that changes, even if long overdue, will take time. But the blacks hear "patience," and think of an excuse and delaying tactics. If we are to reciprocate humanity we have to find common terms to form the covenant for coming together. Too many treaties among nations are written and agreed to with each side putting its own interpretation on the words but with the thoughts and intentions miles apart. Such practices among individuals from different cultures will never reconcile our differences.

Think for a moment of the Los Angeles riots. Though perhaps they were triggered by conditions of the moment, they were caused by things that happened thirty or forty years earlier, deep inside the players. Childhood wounds, never healed, had festered into angry ulcers. Idle songs, mocking jokes, exaggerated incidents, each added another breath to the head of steam which finally blew. New neighborhood police, new apartment projects won't cure a mind that is built up like a house prejudiced and fouled. The good of a new apartment can only be in the good of those who dwell in it.

I have included marriage and family in the discussion of handling human difference because the resolution of the problem begins here. There are those who think that the solution to racial problems is to make no distinctions. Honoring human differences within and between all the races and then coming together in mutual respect is more realistic. Similarly, there are those who believe that minimizing the differences between men and women is the answer to male and female tensions, but you do not get harmony from having everybody play the same note. Neither do you get harmony from having everybody playing his own note irrespective of the notes of others.

Civil law is largely failing to uphold marriage as an institution. Conventional wisdom says make divorce respectable and have blended homes with multiple parents. But such ideas undercut the whole developmental process for learning to work with those who are different from us. If our homes are divided against themselves, the society which is founded upon the home will never embrace tolerance. If we would overcome prejudice, the best place we can possibly start is under our own roofs, in every room of the house.

VIII

▼

THE MUDDLE IN THE MIDDLE
INDIVIDUAL CONSCIENCE IN
ORGANIZED SOCIETY

"All in favor? Opposed? The ayes have it."
After over two years of talk, revise, talk, revise
and talk again, our Operating Policy
Committee's proposal was approved by the
Church's Board of Directors. We had found a
way of helping needy local congregations
without controlling them. I had been one of
the three members of the committee chaired
by the Bishop that had seen it through. All
the drafts, all the discussions were worth it.
We were committed to a decentralized
approach that would enable each

congregation to define its own goals and receive help, but still hold up its head.

Freedom, so precious in the life of the Church, was protected. I didn't want to wait around for the post-meeting rehash. When I got home Ve could read approval with one look.

That night with her head on my shoulder, we savored the sense of accomplishment, the disbelief, and the reality. Her pride reminded me just how much her thoughts and thoughtfulness meant. She had been within it all the way. The steady inspirational heartbeat of the proposal was hers. She cared so much for the freedom of the people of the Church that all I needed to do was work hard for it, and she'd love me.

Less than a year later, without even trying the new policy, the two other committee members came to a committee meeting saying, "The proposal won't work."" They then presented copies of a proposal which completely centralized the policy. I saw all the tools of authoritarianism unfolded paragraph by paragraph. If it wasn't the product of a conscious desire to control, it provided all the tools necessary to achieve it.

I spoke my heart out. Their mouths said that they heard, but their eyes and bodies told the real story. They grew impatient. Obviously they had already decided what would be done and had worked hours behind the scenes to prepare the alternative proposal. The Bishop said that he agreed with me in principle but ended up saying, "It's socialism, but I guess we have to do it." I simply did not see why.

It was a long walk home. There was still a chance that the Board would challenge such a complete reversal, but not much since the momentum was already growing.

During the few weeks before the Board meeting every gap in my thoughts found me hanging between hope and reality. Everywhere I saw reasons to oppose the plan. My concern ran deep. Even if the power were wielded benevolently at first, someone would emerge and abuse it in time. Who was leading this effort towards control?

One morning a leading Board member came in to see me. Without hesitation he said, "I hope that you are not going to speak against the proposal in the Board." I replied, "I wish it were different, but I think I must." His whole body tensed, "If you do, you are not suited to be Secretary of the Church, and I'll see to it." Whether he meant it or not, to me it was raw power and undisguised threat. My body went on red alert, and it only took a moment to say good-bye. If there had been any doubt before, I knew then that I must speak and give my best to the Board.

The day came. He presented the plan. No hands? No questions? My hand went up. I spoke the words which had been going through my head and heart for the past few weeks. Most of the members looked at their hands or nervously checked the papers before them. The Bishop looked at his watch. Called for the vote. Unanimous. As an officer I had no vote. An older man, perhaps wiser, said to me after the meeting, "I agreed with everything you said, but it couldn't be stopped." Another man, a former ambassador, said, "You are so right; all the French did to control Algeria was to centralize the payroll in Paris." At least some understood what I said. But why no response? It was my first real look at the way power can silence a minority, even at times a majority. Many times since then I have seen power and position produce silence. Often it is unintentional, and those who acquiesce fail their uses from unfounded fear. Love is the fire which makes the metal malleable, but courageously held principle hammers out the tools of a strong organization.

That night with Ve's head on my shoulder I kept mouthing the same question in different words. "Why no one?" "They are afraid," she said. Afraid? They are long-experienced well-established businessmen and members of the Church. The new policy seemed to be so clearly contrary to the teachings of the Church. Then it set in. What's wrong with me that I couldn't convince them? Ministers are supposed to be able to lead through teaching true principles. What's wrong with me? As I wrestled with my inadequacies Ve said little. But she was there. She was there. Boy, was that important.

I went to sleep with tears saying, "But it's the Church." In the morning I woke up twice. The second awakening was reason's protest, "No, it was not the Church. The Church is not the organization with all its power struggles, envy and politics. The Church is the Lord's. It doesn't belong to men, particularly not to me. The Church is all those who in their hearts love the Lord and try to work together in His name." Though Ve was never her best in the morning, it was then that she first heard that I would have to think about getting out of Church administration. I could not serve as the administrative secretary in a centralized system. Not only did the committeeman get his policy, he got me.

Usually in our middle years our challenges broaden, and we begin to wrestle more and more with handling differences in the work place and society at large. Management and leadership styles become concerns and choices, but the issues of conscience are still their underpinnings. In organizations, power is effective in dominating only where there is concern for person and fear. Power or authority itself is not the problem. It can be used or abused, to lead or to control.

Some see cross-cultural relations as a power struggle, and I believe they have much truth on their side. But the use and abuse of power are complex in their exercise and effects. If the less powerful yield to fear, they lose their integrity. If they fight, they often sacrifice their own and others' usefulness. Being independently wealthy, the threat of the loss of my job carried little economic fear. But I love my work, and the threat of the loss of my ability to serve as a priest was awesome. I think blacks and other minorities are economically threatened, but this is a shallow threat compared to the deeper threat of the loss of human worth and dignity.

Though I have seen it in many circumstances, I only understand the abuse of power in a limited way. For example, I can have no real conception of the physical fear which reigned for so many years in the South. Most of us cannot possibly imagine the terror of the Jews in Nazi Germany. Few really understand the perils of the inner city. Power can be abused consciously or unconsciously, civilly, economically, socially. Born of the love of dominion, it lusts for any domain. At whatever stage of development a person is, desire for power attacks faith. Trust and acceptance, unless they can be duped, are its enemy. Creativity and inquiry are no friend to it unless harnessed. Idealism threatens it. Tradition and convention are accepted only as servants or slaves. Individualism obviously has no place. Conscience and humanity are only propaganda tools to manipulate and deceive.

Yet in reality the lust for power can only kill the body, never the spirit unless we let it. The spirit does not conquer by winning the power struggle, rather by rising above it. Surely passive resistance taught us that. If black power is not subordinate to a vision of a higher humanity, it too will fail.

Ve took in human relationships with lightning-fast perception. The same forces which centralized the Church were at work in her own family affairs. She saw clearly that this struggle would soon dissolve our bonds to many in the family. Childhood's love and trust, the friendship and memories of youth, would have to be separated from family and church business. She would never be used or manipulated. She knew what she felt was right, and we went forward, not really knowing from day to day where it would lead.

My resignation as Secretary was a turning point in my career. It set the course for my gradually leaving church administration and abandoning all family business ties. I was named Acting Principal of an elementary school, then a teacher of high school religion. I let my name be placed in nomination for Bishop, but even I heard the questions about my "strained" relationship to the most important lay Church leaders. I never took the nomination really seriously except for what it might symbolize to those who nominated me and out of respect for their freedom to nominate as they saw fit. Under the new Bishop I became Dean of the Theological School over objections from at least one family member. But it wasn't worth a fight. After all, it was an academic position. While it might influence the distant future, it was out of the real power loop. The family member even told the Bishop a year later that "He was surprised I hadn't been as bad as he expected."

My role shifted from being presumed to be in the controlling group to being a minority, I hoped one loyal to the Church itself. Some would say it was my choice, and that I knew the consequences when I challenged the system. As I reflect on those who so desperately want to be an accepted part of humanity, I have a lot of empathy, because I so desperately want to be a more accepted part of the Church I love. Often I feel trapped. Minorities who remain in organizations care so much. Is it power the minority races want? Is it just power I want? It is a question we must always ask.

If we feel a part of an organization, our abilities are seen and utilized. Real acceptance only comes if the organization has the wisdom to listen and, even if the minority's thoughts are not mainstream, moderate its decisions accordingly. A friend of mine put the problem beautifully, he said, "I go to the meetings. I try to keep an open mind and remain ready to make a fair judgment. They come in with the decision all packaged and ready for the vote. And I say to myself, 'You did it again. You went to consider and weigh the action. They already knew the outcome.'"

Under such circumstances a minority can use the majority's tactics and lobby ahead of time. Power for power. It can plan, delay, or plot how to drag out implementations. Withdrawing is another choice. Sitting on your hands and saying nothing is another. Still, if you cannot express your thoughts about things you really care about, with some real hope of affecting the outcome, you are terribly alone. The mere forms of acceptance and free discussion are next to meaningless when the chairman looks at his watch and those in the majority shift in their chairs. When the decisions are settled even before the meeting begins, who can blame a Board member for wanting to go home as soon as he can? Particularly if he feels pressured and powerless, he will want to get out. The minority feels that it loses its very soul and integrity if it does not speak up for what it believes. But being a "token" representative, the more you keep your integrity and speak, the more strident your voice seems to sound. Somehow you are called, but who wants to be a token anyway?

I remember one of the last family business meetings we attended. The chairman called for a vote to approve the minutes of the very meeting we were sitting in. The lawyers had prepared the minutes in advance because then the motions "would be in good legal form," and it was simpler.

The leadership of the majority feels that the minority only criticizes. That certainly was true in the family. They felt that they sincerely wanted to listen and yet got no credit from us. Like so many organizations of the time, they espoused participative management, but could not give it its head. There was more talk, but the decisions remained in the same place. The leadership wanted credit for trying to be fair even though it did not seem to us that anything ever changed or even was moderated. "You had a chance to speak, then you should support. If you accept an institution then you need to curtail your individual needs for the sake of the whole." Yet so often we felt that we were simply being tolerated. It is a matter of attitude. For a minority to be respected and feel respect requires consummate leadership which from conscience really endorses the God-given worth of each member. Even though he had many qualities of a benevolent authoritarian, Ve's father really strove for such a role. We on both sides in the next generation faltered.

Participation was perhaps a sincere effort to find a way out. Deming and Covey and you name them only answer if the mission lifts us out of ourselves. But it is more than being part of a team. We need a call to personal integrity before a God of love to release our real human potential. Love disciplined by self-evident and revealed truth is big enough to allow all to find their place and thrive.

Consent is a tricky thing. If you ask for it, the majority enjoys giving it, because they can do it with little concern for control. Obviously, a vociferous and fanatical minority should not be able to filibuster the decisions. Wise government must try to eliminate situations where anyone feels that he or she must subordinate fundamental integrity to someone else's decision. If you reinforce and lead from principle, then at least there is internal agreement and all can identify with the underlying motive and purpose.

Many leaders woo the majority and feel that they have done their job when they attain majority support. But they have lost the potential growth and commitment which can come from hammering out differences. There are tremendous potential rewards if we consciously and creatively learn to accommodate our differences according to the Divine Rules of Humanity and draw out the individual's unique abilities. The greater good is served when the talents of all are tapped.

Young as I was, I felt that my father-in-law really wanted to hear my views on both the Doctrine and the Church's policy. We were moving into more "scientific management" as his leadership faded. Statistically our communities with schools, like the one I grew up in, were growing more rapidly than other church centers. The proposal was that the center of the Church financially sponsor the development of new local church communities. He worried about taking away the incentives and freedom of the local people. I understood his concerns from principle, but felt that if we did it "right" we could still preserve freedom. Several times he cornered me on the issue, and we spent a number of hours, one on one, in the upstairs living room discussing it—even to his fears as to those individuals who might use the situation unwisely. We did not entirely agree, particularly at first. But we came to understanding through mutual respect. He let me see what he stood for and why, and I loved him for it.

But not everyone had or could have such a close relationship with this remarkable man. The more removed he was from the give and take, the more he appeared to support only traditional and conventional patterns. Under a single authority, even if benevolent, independence and freedom are too often curtailed, often unintentionally by the leader and frequently through the inhibitions of the followers.

When his era passed, not surprisingly both the family company and the Church moved rather quickly into a more pragmatic or scientific leadership pattern, together with a sort of juggling aristocracy. In his day the proud motto of the company was, "Profit with honor." It was mentioned frequently at company and family meetings. In just a short time the family meetings became choreographed, and over drinks afterwards the oft-repeated joke was, "What's the purpose of a pickle factory?" When you replied, "To make pickles," the response was, "No, to make money."

This pragmatism was only part of the story. There were many family members in the next generation who were not business-minded and who relied upon a few to recommend both company and church policy. They saw loyalty to the company as one with loyalty to the church. As the company tended to business more and more, the church was urged to become more business-like.

In church affairs the wealthy are often unaware of the impact of their position. It is so easy in a board or on a committee to say from affection, "If you do this, I will pay for it." Yet for many followers implicit in that statement is, "If you don't do this my way, I won't pay for it." And a doubt can be sown as to whether the support of other uses will suffer if the speaker does not get his way.

Gradually the church slipped into a kind of aristocratic leadership by the wealthy—particularly the leaders of the wealthy families. But such leadership must inform and win the consent of the governed on the basis of their loyalty to a common mission and the principles which support it, or it too will hold the followers to an imposed or self-imposed conventional business-like response. Over time, people who are striving for individual consent will rebel in resentment.

To put this in a broader context, consider the transition from Hoover Republicanism to the Roosevelt era. Roosevelt used the emerging medium of radio to pit the people against the "economic royalists." With charisma and dynamism he appealed to every man's desire to manage himself. Through the labor movement he turned them against the management "aristocrats."

But just as an individual does not gain independence simply by being pitted against convention, neither did the people gain real freedom and responsibility through the movement towards the apparently more participative democracy that Roosevelt offered.

An uninformed electorate can be manipulated by a charismatic leader who either stands for principle, or appears to. Many

almost instinctively see a call to higher law
and principle as the way to freedom and
responsibility.   Roosevelt,   Eisenhower,
Goldwater, and Kennedy, each in his own way
seems to illustrate the power of this appeal to
rise above conventional behavior. But so far
the principles have not risen to sufficient
height or gained sufficiently broad acceptance
to win that potential human release.

The media must bear some responsibility
for this failure. Seeing the danger of sheep
merely following the charismatic, they have
attacked the messengers again and again,
and yet failed to uphold the value of the message. In their supposed search for the truth,
they have attacked the bonds of convention
and put nothing in its place. Their ratings go
up if they create "news," rather than just
report it. So they feed society what it wants
to hear.

The universities too must bear some
responsibility. In a supposed effort to encourage independent thought, professors attack
many of society's conventions and replace
them with weak arguments for shades of gray
and the conventions of situation ethics.

Many editorial policies are the product of
the university and cynically attack conventional behavior. They mock leadership and
each other until the electorate, uninformed
and bored with the bickering, runs the risk of
being merely manipulated on whim.

The courts too have spawned a doctrine of separation of church and state in such a way as to drive a wedge between religious principles and the actual practice of government. They have then tried to fill the gap by handing down socially motivated decisions. Perhaps most threatening to society and spiritual maturation, they have increasingly turned domestic law over to social theory and psychiatry. For example, no-fault divorce has become an invitation to license, not to freedom, and judges determine such things as custody more and more under the influence of social workers and psychologists.

Many churches also teach politics and form political action groups rather than teaching the spiritual values to lead their followers and the leaders of the country to the True Source of independence. In many cases non-doctrinal pablum has replaced the nurturing food for which we could truly bow our heads and be thankful.

If the way to responsible individual spirituality is acknowledgment of true and God-given principles, how can we grow if our political leaders, the media, the universities, the courts, and even the clergy serve up platitudes and blandness? Is it any wonder that in their religious development so many stop somewhere between conventional behavior and rebelling and griping about governmental controls and

society's lack of integrity? We see something
of this struggle in the ambivalence which
the nation shows regarding moral scandal
in our leadership. It is easier to simply rebel
than make a moral judgment.

Today, rebelling against the mockery of
apparent democracy and participation, the
trend is towards consensus building, in the
country, in society, in the church, and even in
our homes. If leadership does its job, the theory goes, then everybody should "win." But in
the matters of right and wrong, good and evil
can't both win. We may properly build consensus as to how the principles are to be
applied, but the principles which lead individual conscience to speak with one voice are not
born of consensus but are God-given.

Can anyone seriously believe that the
dilemma of race relations can be solved by
consensus building? Will human beings really
be brought together by taking surveys of what
each one wants? Where is the call to think of
others? Charity involves subordination of self,
not to the will of others but to God. We all
win—and human relationships thrive—only if
we are drawn together by a commitment to
higher principles and the greater good.

Polls and surveys are often the tools of
consensus building. They let us know what
people think and feel, and all too frequently
simply what they want. The thought is too often
shallow and the feelings self-centered and

superficial. The results are often programmed by the design of the questions. The analyses are not expressions from fundamental principles, nor do they provide the opportunity to discuss and share the fundamental issues which underlie any wise decision. Our seemingly limitless use of surveys and polls provides a pretty clear picture of where our faith development has stalled.

Developmentally, my church as an organization is threatened by radical individualism. It can revert to human authoritarianism and in all probability die. It can try to thread its way through its dilemmas and build consensus and compromises in the hope of holding the diverse elements together and preserving peace when there is no peace. Or it can find a way of using the authority of God's teachings to inspire individual conscience and allow God to provide unity.

On our better days, many of us really seem to want to reach and reach again. On our worse days we hold another committee meeting or write another policy or manual, because we can't trust the real human mission to provide answers as we move along. As we shun what is against God and grow in spirit, we will discover more and more who our God really is.

Leadership should involve a clarion call for the group to be better than we are as individuals. Instead, we divide into small groups with reporters. Such groups are among the tools of consensus building. But the reporting process often gives the appearance of consensus without real consent. Leadership is said to come from the bottom up and is believed to be better than the authoritarian leading from the top down. But what happened to leadership which involves top and bottom—all—inquiring into the will of the One Who made us in the first place, whether that will is expressed in the order of nature or the words of Revelation?

Our vision of our mission defines the limitations of participative consensus building. If it is a living inquiry, creative growth occurs. Mouthing freedom and that everybody wins, yet consciously or unconsciously manipulating merely human opinions is no answer. The opinion surveyors and opinion makers, the image builders, the masters of the spin, the speech writers, the big contributors, the lobbyists, and a host of other like forces support an entrenched bureaucracy which hems in and molds leadership. Leaders become products of the popular conventional forces of the system. Rarely do they really articulate visions and aspirations which go beyond lip service to the Creator. And even those who articulate a moral or spiritual vision too often cannot deliver it or, worse, simply use it for their own ends.

I have described examples from my experience. Whether you are a manager or a union member, a Republican or Democrat, black or white, male or female, no matter what church you belong to or don't belong to, I'll bet you could describe similar feelings or experiences.

Of course ideals are espoused. We demand at least lip service to our roots. But these ideals are countered by such slogans as "Politics is the art of the possible."

I have attended meeting after meeting where we brainstormed and reported and pasted sheets of notes on the wall. I've had plenty of appointments that had very effective time management: i.e. short.

Individually and in private, active listening techniques are frequently used. Many of us in a minority know that the interview is about to end when we hear the words, "I hear you." Our feelings are supposed to be soothed, but our proposals are filed. My boss has even said apologetically that, "He had handled me badly." But it is not a matter of handling individuals. Unless we share articulated and common principles, consensus building for all its appearances curtails the growth of individual responsibility and conscience.

When consensus building does not lead to support of the desired decision, leadership often asserts its authority and the minority is told to "Process their anger."

Again, think of how these forces have been applied to the relation of husband and wife. For years the husband was presumed to be the authoritarian—benevolent, of course. Then with scientific precision the sex act was dissected into erotic areas and sequences. Then we moved neat democratic processes into the home. Still later we espoused permissiveness, each walking their own paths, asserting their "selves." Those who were insecure in these roles wrote contracts and lists. Still others, the more advanced, use all kinds of communication and consensus building techniques so both partner's "win." Where is the call to a covenant freely consented to before God? Who is calling us to act according to rules above humanly contrived conventions and practices?

Marriage is not a compromise. It is not a consensus built through psychological techniques. It is an intimate mutual dedication to our neighbor and to God. The closer partners come together in love freely given, the more their sense of individuality is enhanced. When our marriages live by the self-evident truths our founders held in common, we will find a renewed vision as a nation.

Our Creator put untold potential delights into the relationship of husband and wife. He made it possible for two people from very different perspectives to freely cultivate love and trust, mutual ideals, common traditions, and a common eternal vision. In the Divine scheme our marriages can teach us to handle human difference in a supremely rewarding way. With the integrity of a vision bigger than we are, true marriages can renew our country and restore the mission of humanity. Because God is One, we can be one—if we will.

Most in America today are caught between their desire to break out as individuals and their recognition that somehow they are responsible to others. There is a way. We must discover not only our inalienable rights but our God-given talents and responsibility to Him. A good place to begin is an honest look at ourselves, the impact of our past, the strengths and problems of our present and our hopes for the future. Are they worthy of what our God intends for us?

IX

▼

ADVERSITY
GRIEF AND GROWTH

Ve had a slight fever and headache and had stayed in bed for the last couple of days. She hated doctors, but I, uncertain of her agreement, issued the edict, "If you're not better tomorrow we're going to the doctor." The next day I made the appointment. I came and asked her to get dressed. She gave me an unusual look of compliance, stood up, and collapsed in my arms. I carried her to the car.

Two days of tests later the diagnosis came through: a brain tumor, both lobes of the brain, inoperable, six months to live. "Could anything be done?" "She might tolerate X-ray, coming in every other day. She'd lose her hair, and probably be sick." "What would we gain?" "Four to six weeks." "Any hope of a cure?" "Perhaps one in a million. I've never heard of it."

They had temporarily shrunk the tumor, so though she was slow she was coherent. As always, we talked it over, but the decision seemed obvious to both of us. She would stay at home, and we'd make her comfortable there.

One of my first thoughts was to try to anticipate all the things I should do with the seven children. The youngest boy was nine. After tolerating my questions for an hour or so, she finally said, "Bob, we can't possibly know what their circumstances will be in the future. I trust you. That's enough."

The next six months were unreal. I never heard one complaint, just patient trust and acceptance. Much I have simply blocked out. Still, I remember the overpowering dark waves of grief—most of which I sealed up inside. I remember the hours of being there, not really thinking, only half feeling—but there. I remember her hesitatingly placing her feet one after another to get out and see the fall coloring. She had written dedications in all the kids' special books and was determined to write a dedication in a book for our youngest son. Three or four sentences took about an hour a day for over a week. What force of will!

The nurse, seeing my fading too, suggested that I sleep in the guest room for my sake. The next day the nurse asked me to come back. Ve had told her firmly, "I do not want the kids ever to think of us in separate beds."

The fifth month brought coma. I stayed on. It did something for me—and I think for her. The border between unconsciousness and consciousness is so undefined. The tumor apparently got most of the pain centers and she needed little medication.

Late one afternoon we knew the time was close. She had her head on my shoulder. It seemed to be getting heavier. I recited some of the Scripture she loved to hear. There was something there whether she heard or not. Her breathing faltered—faded—faltered—stopped—started—then stopped altogether. I said the prayer, lay there awhile, and then called the nurse.

At the gathering after the funeral I tried to explain, "When you don't know whether to pray for her to live or pray for her release, all you can do is turn it over to the Lord."

Half of me was gone. Strangely, it seemed as if my will and inspiration, so much "me" had dried up. If we were not still close, I felt there was no future. But how? We had always worked together with the kids and the church. As the days passed, I realized that the only way to be close was to go forward with the things we both loved. Work became and still is my antidote to loneliness. Perhaps at first it was an escape, but it is much more than that. In a subtle way I discovered that she was still with me. It is something like the way I felt her presence when I was at work and she was at home. It is a different presence, in a sense deeper, but still very real. I do not ask myself anymore what she would do when this or that comes up. I still feel her confidence in whatever I decide. I confess that sometimes when things get really tough with the kids I just lean back and say, "O.K. Ve, you take over." And funny as it sounds, it sort of brings a trusting and affectional perspective.

I remember coming home from a meeting perhaps two months after she had died. Unthinking, I said to myself, "I must tell Ve about that." In my head I realized that I was going to slant the telling a bit in my favor, to show I had said the right thing. Then I said to myself, "But she sees through all that now." Then I took a few more steps and thought, "She probably always did."

One of the feminine qualities I particularly appreciate in her is her ability to recognize my limitations without undermining my confidence. She shows loyalty and love despite my faults. Somehow she inspires me, without any thought of personal ambition. She always puts in her views without hesitation, but waits for me to make the decisions in my work

and then supports them. She never pictured
me in high office even when I was nominated
but was unswerving in her support of me as
potentially someone of integrity who would follow his lights wherever they led. For our
sakes, I have tried to never be moved from
standing for what I truly believe is right. Oh,
she reminds me when I need to be softened or
need to show more human warmth and concern. She is there for someone who perhaps
failed adequately to express warmth for the
one he loves most, but whose bumbling is
accepted and understood for all its lacks. I put
these things in the present tense, not to make
them mystical, but because I feel them as a
more powerful force than mere memory. Her
conscience and mine, looking to the common
source in the Word and prayerfully seeking
one God and His love, not were, but *are* essential to a process I earnestly hope is continuing.

Clearly, if eternal life means anything, she
is the same Ve I love and will love when I join
her. Her physical presence is gone. Her
words and actions cannot speak to me or
touch me. But her uniquely feminine
inspiration, her sphere of affection is there.
It moves me more powerfully in a sense
because it is unhindered by physical
limitations and awkward self-conscious and
inadequate gestures, those stumbling words
or self-imposed silences. I still need her
because she is so completely different from

me. She has everything important in life that I am missing. As a male, my whole approach to life is different. If, when we meet again, she needs what I have to offer, then a uniquely human and eternally loving relationship will be sealed—in the name of love, in the name of God.

Differences, male and female, national, racial, are all harmonized from deep within by choice; they are not imposed from without. We are brought together by His great love in the light of His infinite wisdom. We are confronted deep within our being to love and be loved, to be truly human from God or merely human from ourselves.

There were hundreds of things as a man that I could not do for the kids, perhaps particularly the girls. Looking into their big questioning blue eyes as their little insides cramped, what could I say about the promise of menstruation? I turned to aunts and relatives to help me feed that precious innocence. In quiet moments when they too worried, in its own way having an angel mother nurtured them at the same time it challenged. At times it was an almost unachievable ideal, as it still is for me, but at other times the thought of her was almost as if she ran her fingers gently through their hair again.

I had not bothered changing the furnishings of our bedroom, including the set-up of her dressing table. Others had come and put away her clothes. Several years later my then teen-aged son came into the room, pulled the stopper from the perfume bottle and smelled it. Then he said quietly, "I like to smell that, because it makes me close to Mama." She was with him, too.

Some may call it memory, but when love is involved it's much more than that. It's an awesome, mysterious, supportive presence. It hangs in the balance between the real and the unreal. But if your love says that you need it, it's real—so real.

When a spouse dies, some say the remaining parent must be a mother and father to their children. In the day-to-day cooking and bundling-them-off-to-school sense I know what they mean. But I believe the best possible way for me to "be a mother to them," is to love their mother deeply. The same precious human qualities which hold me fast can be seen, respected, and loved by the children, even when their mother is not present in the room.

It was interesting that one of the first things the older girls requested was to fire Mildred, our daytime maid. They had a real affection for her, and I do not think their request came easily, but they realized that if she stayed she would try to fill in. Circumstance had called them to responsibility, and they wanted the opportunity to take it. With my work, the kids were often left to take care of themselves, and the older girls to take care of the younger ones, whether they wanted it or not. I realized that if they took greater responsibility they needed greater freedom. Of course there were moments, but they gained a kind of reliance on the Lord and each other on a path that surely I would not have chosen for them, but "Who's going to argue with the Lord?"

Sometimes they got more than they bargained for—particularly when Grandma got too old to live alone. With a white lie, I convinced her to come "help" me with the kids. The reality was that I was asking the kids to help look after Grandma: to turn off the stove when she left it on, to help her find the things she was perpetually losing, to pick up the endless things she dropped, and patiently clean up the broken dishes when she helped. They even gently reminded her if her clothes got too many stains from unsteady arthritic hands at the table. It wonders me how they did it so well.

Given their gentle affectional response, it hurt when Grandma would tell me so all could hear, "You know, that girl is lying to you." Or since Grandma couldn't take the stairs, it saddened me to see the youngest boy come home from school, say "Hi," and then run upstairs to his room. It was his way of coping with the refrain of "that boy" assertions. But to this day that same boy, now a married man, remembers his tender sympathy for his confused Grandma who saw "ghost clouds" across the valley, and at the same time would shake her head and say, "I know they are not real."

When after a few years Grandma had a minor stroke, my sister, then retired as a nurse, took her across the country to her home for her final care. None of us would have planned the Grandma era, but it helped us think beyond our hurts and remember there are others. Feeling like the victim and turning inward is no cure for grief.

You cannot love without knowing grief, because grief is an opportunity to change and think of others. Surely a loving God does not will suffering, but He permits it as a means to break our selfish tendencies and grow. We can learn so much from hurt. It makes us think and invites change. Minorities need not be debilitated victims. Toynbee had a point. The spirit of a bound people can grow through natural adversity, if we let it.

It was some time before sunrise. The phone rang. My son-in-law's struggling voice said, "It's Erin. Someone broke into her house. She's been raped. She's at the hospital, but they say she'll be all right." I just said, "I'm coming right away."

The kids and I have turned to each other since their Mom died almost twenty years ago. Unusual bonds have formed, perhaps as each of them in his or her own way has reflected a little piece of their mother. I have appreciated their warm ties of confidence and have shared confidence with them. I am privileged to know some of their deeper dreams, and they know some of mine.

The whole three-hour drive I cried and I cried out. She had nurtured her virginity for years. It was to be a special gift to the man she would love. Hell itself broke out and violated her. Anger—we've got to get him. Despair—who can bring back her trust? When the heart asks "Why?" the question is too deep for any ready answer. Thought doesn't put warmth back into the soul; only love can.

We spent the next days putting patches back onto her spirit wherever we could. The winter of shock began to thaw, but spring looked pretty dismal. We both went back to the tick-tock of work.

I returned home feeling deserted. The phone rang. It was the first friend who had heard of my return. I felt his outrage. It could not equal, but in some sense justified my own. It helped that others were angry too. I appreciated his friendship. But then came the question, "Was he black?" What possible difference could it make to the violation and horror of the crime? I knew she had been blindfolded in the dark at knifepoint. She might not know for sure. Was that why I had not asked?

He was caught after assaulting three more victims. I never realized how important his being caught and punished would be to my daughter. Not for revenge. But now she could let go any false and lingering doubts about guilt. Society itself would judge, condemn and punish.

Victims of any kind of injustice cry out for the judgment and support of society. If it is not there, they doubt themselves. Victimization of any individual or group undermines confidence and a sense of worth. Was he black? I did not want to ask.

It hurts that when he was caught he turned out to be black. My hope for improved race relations in the next generation has a daughter who finds it hard to feel safe around black men. She is fighting it, but.... Why do these things happen?

The Lord who is truly Human and loving can never will such things. But though He is all-powerful, He must permit them for the sake of the good and the love which can come out of them. It is just possible that my daughter is up to the challenge to work through her relation to blacks in a unique and powerfully forgiving way. She seems to recognize that it is not a black and white thing, but simply evil. We all need to really count on the Lord's wisdom and love.

Most indications are that rape is a power thing. Surely it gives us a look at some of the grossest and basest depths of which we are capable. I will never justify it, but I will ask, is perhaps the prostitution of black women by whites a cause of the rape of white women by black men? When God permits violence and rape between the races, is He perhaps calling us to stop and think? He can't change our hearts unless something brings us to ask Him. During His life here, even He became a victim so that He could reveal His Divine love to us.

*　　　　*　　　　*

For years I served the Church in administration. But the more committees I endured while squirming in my chair, the more I saw the priest's real work as service. Church bureaucracy can so easily become separated, even divorced, from the people of the Church. High-sounding bureaucratic solutions produced by a Church hierarchy are no substitute for the heart, hands and words of a caring pastor.

As my term as Dean of the Theological School drew to its close, I saw an opportunity in a neighboring community to try to build a congregation. A number of families loved sending their children to the parochial schools, but simply could not afford to live in the University Town itself. I saw the opportunity to be a pastor again—serving these "blue collar" members and reaching out to others. Though you would never know it from my career, the real reason I became a minister was to be a pastor. Curiously, the more I got back into the work, the closer I felt to Ve. Closer I think, because I was closer to the real reason she married me. Only God can make a man human. But He uses our wives to do it.

As the congregation grew, we built our own building, largely with our own hands. As we hammered and painted together, tremendously diverse characters found treasures in each other. We became a congregation. I said later of the building's several warts and numerous bumps, that they were unimportant in the building even as they were in our neighbors, because we saw the underpinning love behind each. It became a joke that if a person attended church twice, I put them to work. One lady inquired about the church while we were still worshiping in the Manse, and I explained that we were painting after the service. She arrived to her first service with bib overalls and a paint brush and has been working for the Church ever since.

One of the Korean theologs and I formed a plan for a bicultural Church. The Korean churches in this country try to hold onto their traditions, yet after one or two generations often no longer even understand the language. Our hope was that by holding an English service with social life following and then holding a Korean service, we would be able to blend the congregations socially, teach each other language and cross-cultural values.

The challenge seemed too great. When I left the congregation, the theolog, now an ordained minister, planned to start an independent congregation in Philadelphia. But his people urged him to continue the way we were. If we can really work through the challenge, and honor and share cultural values, there is much to gain. Think for example of the traditional Korean discipline and its potential moderating effect on the modern American family, and vice versa. We could learn so much from their respect for elders and order. I do not have answers, but I am convinced that religion can play a vital role in helping immigrants to find a truly human home here. So much can be done in the name of God.

The Church called my son-in-law to serve an English-speaking congregation in South Africa. They now have seven children of their own there. Those kids have an opportunity to observe a country trying to rise to an unimaginably difficult task. The schools are integrating. They have some black friends. They have sometimes been the only whites at Church camp. They felt left out of almost all conversation, which was in Zulu.

The country itself has such a long way to go. Many in South Africa are afraid. My family, particularly my daughter, is too. But good things are happening. The Lord leads through our intentions. He identifies more with our efforts than our achievements. Certainly my grandchildren are being exposed to circumstances I never dreamt for them. But they are also being given tremendous opportunities to grow. The plans are that the family will return to the U. S. in another year. Though my daughter and her husband have seven children, they felt called to adopt a little abandoned Zulu baby. I have not seen her yet, but I have seen pictures of her siblings holding her or feeding her. I see a very special kind of bonding and trust in their eyes. The whole family will want her to be a full part and yet know her heritage. I am confident that she will find a home in their family because they are accustomed to working through issues. She and they will have temptations to face as she lives and grows in their sphere and works through her ties to her heritage. Still, all of us have a portion of the bread of life which is to be eaten with bitter herbs. None of us will reach tolerance, much less working together, without struggle.

The ambivalent drive to recapture and defend cultural uniqueness can potentially become a taproot that anchors our whole perspective on life. On the other hand it can be a shameful and misunderstood exposure titillating a fascination with something little understood but nevertheless exploited.

I remember some "traditional" Zulu dancers in a park in Johannesburg. Those dancers, stripped to the waist, tuning their movements to the past, must perceive the sweaty lust in the crowd of white tourists as they watch and fantasize. Is this using or abusing the past?

Revisiting our roots may have to be an individual quest within the culture itself in order to kindle the just pride it deserves. Perhaps we must closet ourselves when we revisit those almost-still fingers that strum the strings of a past long silent, but deeply moving.

As we explore more deeply, people are tempted to say, "I know how you feel." Yet I know that they *don't* know, any more than I know what paces their hearts. The Simpson trial gave many of us the opportunity to stop and think. One of my black friends particularly hoped that it would get the races talking together significantly. He had learned from childhood not to expect an even hand from the police. Therefore he saw in the trial an obvious exposure of racism in law enforcement. At last, he thought, wc can really look at what goes on. I focused on the evidence as I understood it, and I saw justice being distorted by playing upon racism rather than considering the facts. He felt that I lacked concern for the real moral issue. I felt that media-driven emotionalism was a poor climate for resolving anything.

My friend and I talk now of these things. The urgency is gone. Yet I wonder—will the resolution best come with urgency, triggered by the ratings-driven voices of the media? Perhaps a renewal of our individual covenant with each other and with our Maker is a surer answer.

When we view another culture from the accepted values of our own, we are lucky if we penetrate beyond mere curiosity. But if as individuals we have learned to look for the God-given gifts of others with a mind to dance something of life's rhythm with them, then we may learn. It will be a mental exercise at first; then perhaps it will deceptively entice us; but it will be rare indeed if it urges us to the profound depths of our common humanity.

We can't separate influences from experiences, but must learn to accept influence in order to understand our place in life. Stages of growth combine and mystify sometimes.

I believe it is very good to stand proud of all that makes us who we are. But I pray that even in the face of countless un-probed differences, we will grant others their pride in their inner being as an image of their Maker.

Occasionally I have been invited to meet with a small church group in central Philadelphia. I deliberately drive an older pick-up truck from the farm to avoid ostentation and the risk of theft. As noted before, our church has turned out to be WASP, as I believe many churches have, quite unintentionally. I ask myself, "Could I serve such a church?" My answer is, "No." I hate the city. I am accustomed to a lifestyle too far beyond that of those whom I would serve. And, frankly, I would be afraid—too scared to be effective. I don't think it is a race thing. I respect the people and they accept me on my visits. I honestly can't say what's going on inside. These are the kinds of things I think we need to ponder.

In this world we only gain the tools for perfection, often through adversity. But we will be perfected to eternity in a world where the challenge to express love replaces adversity as the stimulus to growth.

Today I give memorial services for one friend after another. These have their sadness. But on the other hand, with each graduation heaven becomes more real and more to be desired. The kingdom of a loving God both within and as a heavenly goal is the great universal Promise at the end of this life's struggle. When I think of my friends' eternal life, I know them better for who I believe they are. And with each passing I know myself better as well.

The arthritis cries out. The drives on the golf course shorten. Some say I am more patient. I wonder if I am just getting tired. On bad days things become so important—the smaller they are, the bigger they seem. But on good days I reflect—the trust, the sense of wonder, the dreams, the trials, the confidence in justice, the sense of being a part of a bigger whole, all shout out purpose and peace. Then I know for sure that while I in no way have all the answers, there is One who surely does. Because He is Divinely Human, a God of love, wisdom, and eternal care, He calls each of us to image that humanity to each other.

Heaven, this grand universal of faith, is a Kingdom of varied and harmonized uses. Mutual service is the key to eternal growth and truly human fulfillment. It does not depend upon bodily resurrection, nor is the individual swallowed up as in Nirvana. But founded on every individual's ruling intent, heaven provides a place for all those who have with sincere intent followed their diverse religious paths.

X

---▼---

WHAT NEXT?

Heaven, The Eternal Universal Which Accommodates Diversity

As human beings, we either accept death as the end of our existence, or we postulate something beyond. Ordinary sense experience cannot answer our questions. We depend rather upon our faith to describe the hereafter. The more the character of the life after death is based upon our life here, the more responsibility it places upon us. If with death we suddenly and dramatically change who we are, the life hereafter will be unreal. Our vision of heaven may become a satisfying emotional escape, but it will have little continuity with or impact on our day-to-day decisions here. It is impossible then to imagine a heaven where we do not trust, do not have ideals, do not live and work with others, do not feel love as our very life, in short where we are not the full measure of ourselves. As the Divine purpose of life, heaven must encompass and sustain all the stages of faith as far as each of us, in our own way, comes to know them. That means it is impossible to imagine our being part of a heaven where there is not a mature acceptance of human differences. I hope when/if we all get there that I will see Nagashima-san, Yong, Kofi, Ankra, Cristovao, Maseko, and the whole spread of my friends from throughout the world.

But I look forward particularly to being with that special confidante and partner with whom I shared my life. If sex difference and the consequent need and love that we feel for the opposite sex is God-given, is it not also eternal?

If our view of life hereafter includes the possibility of an eternal relationship with the one we love, it profoundly influences our day-to-day life here. My wife died many years ago, but my looking forward to being with her again has influenced profoundly how I have lived my life. It is not just the thought that one day we will be together again. We live right now according to what and whom we love. In so far as our married love is mutual, it influences and affects everything I do. Our love for each other influenced my life when she was physically present. But just so far as I love her, it influences my life now. It is my most sincere prayer that that love will continue to influence every activity of my eternal life. She is an integral part of my hopes and my happiness, of me.

Years ago I used to phone Ve before I would start to walk home from my office across the park. I would see her slim figure swaying gently as she came to meet me. I love the lilt in her walk, so much her. My whole spirit tuned as we approached. Many is the time I imagine her coming towards me as we meet again in one of heaven's fields. Even now when I think of her, I feel close, but *then* I will really be home again. I will see her, hear her voice, feel the brush of her hair in the breeze. Her subtle presence means so much *now*, it is hard to write of the wonder and anticipation of *then*. The love and inspiration I feel now from her is what I live for. In one sense, it can't be any more precious. Yet it can become a renewed and present reality. It can be fruitful and multiply in ever-unfolding growth and usefulness. The action and reaction will be rich and open, where now it is a glass darkly, a subtle and powerful sphere, yearning and vital, but also wanting. All these years we have been together, yet not. There will be much to say, and yet so little need to say it. Together.

I always felt deeply trusted and realistically accepted, an intimate and important part of her life. Of course there were thick times when she couldn't take me and went on long walks by herself. When confronted with the "I wants" of life, it was obvious that if we were to be really joined together, only God could do it. It takes miracles for God to overcome selfishness. But reconciliation came more and more easily as we both prayed for it.

She brought to our home the desire for family worship. She sparked regular Church attendance. Her probing inquiries and statements lifted our conversation to ponder values and uses in human terms. For example, she loved to do laundry. Why? Because it was a special time to think individually about each member of her family as she folded and stacked their clothes. She reached to guide the depth of our lives, not just the superficialities. Her presence was a tangible force for justice. She cared for the house for the sake of the home she fostered. Her sphere promoted warmth and harmony. Her questions and inquiring mind prodded me to the boundary of wonder. Her comments like gentle waves undercut my proud sandcastles when I lost sight of the True Foundation Rock. But her sustaining trust made patterns in the sand and preserved the beauty even of the tiniest detail. She made our life—the retrospect of the past, the warmth of the present, the hope for the future.

Being separated by that semi-permeable membrane we call death, more than ever I pray that she knows I cannot live without her friendship. Eternal life without her is nothing. Did she know while she was here how much I depended on her? Did she know the extent of my love? Too rarely I spoke of it. Yet she was so tuned to the unspoken that I suspect she knew. Love always seemed to be there in the measure it was needed. At times we cried together in desperate frustration with ourselves. But we counted the victories, not the defeats.

In our middle years the births were not easy as we struggled hard for the causes we saw clearly. There were both physical and spiritual miscarriages. Perhaps at times the zeal was too sure of itself. But together we will discover the balance and find true inspiration with one voice, one shoulder.

Her point of view is a profound contrast to mine, but in trying to be useful there is a conception of life that neither could produce alone. All our joy and wonder when our babies took their first breath is matched and even surpassed when a previously unseen opportunity for use is conceived and born. Something of those new births has continued in subtle, mysterious, and often unsuspected ways during our natural separation. There is so much to do I haven't time to long for death, but I know that the intense longing to be openly with her again is accepted by the very God who came into the world to support our humanity and capacity to love.

I have tried to share these feelings, however inadequately, because I am convinced that they depend upon the eternal uniqueness of the male and the female. God created complementary beings, each with unique qualities which are desperately needed by the other. These mutual needs are the origin of the tenderest love we can ever know. God did not—He could not—create one to dominate the other, or there could be no such genuine love. Yet it is complete and total folly to think men and women are the same. The more we lovingly celebrate and appreciate our differences, the more we are filled with the eternal wonder of our love for our partners. The unrestrained struggle for power and dominion is the culprit, not male/female difference.

Imagine the impact on courtship if forever was the hope driving our choice. Poets sing of forever. We may even murmur it when we propose. But imagine the impact on marriage and the family if the vision behind it was husband and wife working together actively and freely serving God and their neighbor, forever.

I have spent a lifetime of counseling people who are in troubled marriages. Ve and I had our share of moments. Many cultures have cultivated a dominant role for men. Paul's apparent teaching was applied with devastatingly sad consequences to the Western world. There has been unconscionable and one-sided abuse. But denial of difference is no answer. To be needed, we must have qualities someone else lacks. Possessing those qualities does not make us better, but it does make us useful and desirable. God created male and female to become perfect loving and eternal partners. I expect to need Ve forever—and I hope she needs me.

"Male and female created He them." But what of other created differences? Variety enhances human life. It provides an unlimited opportunity to renew our need and appreciation for each other. Human interaction can be eternally invigorating, because we are different. Different appearance, different temperament, different affections and thoughts, both the created and the acquired, perfect human relationships when properly regarded. We can learn to work together like all the parts in the human body, each unique yet serving one Divine end. We can find lasting joy in freely conjoining our efforts with others' with the ruling purpose of making others happy.

It is impossible to imagine a heaven where we are not ourselves. It is impossible to imagine the perfection of heaven without all retaining our unique differences. But the residue of prejudice still clinging to our natural reactions will diminish and disappear. All the seemingly important distinctions of this world fade as we learn to look at the reality of humanity and work together because we love working together and being together.

The people of heaven have made their own the same tender love and trust that they knew as infants. They love and trust each other because they want to. All their surroundings are alive with wonder. They can confidently explore that world like children, unaware of the pressures of time. Their loves lead them to discoveries as far as their imaginations can carry them, unfettered by fixed spatial limitations. There is limitless variety to see, hear, feel, smell, and taste. Their experiences are bound only by their ability to assimilate. And being useful to the full extent of their ability, they earn a complete sense of belonging and being accepted by God and each other. They feel their life and their loves as their own beyond the dreams of any youth. They are themselves, not through reacting against heavenly society but through free and loving cooperation. The more they love, the more they become themselves, and the more universal the impact of their lives on others. They simply could not be more free, because their highest concern is the freedom of others. Here is the fulfillment of that human potential which began so long ago with our first breath here on earth.

But there is more. Toddlers learn the meaning of the word "No," and respect it from fear, even if only the fear of their parents' displeasure. They learn order. The order of heavenly society is sustained because the angels have learned to say "No" from within. The habit of controlling self is so deep-seated that there is no fear of punishment, no feeling of imposed restraint. Each one is valued and seen as a treasure from God. People don't struggle to express themselves and are readily understood. They speak openly from love, and all understand. The potential seeds of prejudice are replaced by a delight in discovery and spontaneous understanding.

In this world, imagination serves true character. It is the tool of invention. Its pictures are the paradigms of hope. In heaven it serves to form the objects which surround us. These are not fleeting fantasies, but real appearances whose quality reflects the great constant of our love for others. Childhood's imaginary world seems so real at times. But it can't compare to the realities of heaven, where everything is matched perfectly to our life's loves. Neighbors show their love; we are inspired to show ours. As neighbors we serve and are served. Mutual usefulness is the way of heavenly life.

Think of a world where we support the loves and efforts of each other, where the rule of life is that individual variety perfects the harmony of the whole, because God Himself is present. His Divine love is universal and reaches out to all humanity. When we truly love Him, we love all His uniquely created gifts to our fellow man. We love with all our hearts whatever we see to be of God in our neighbor. Love perceives. Truth sees. Truth defines differences and then urges relationships in that light. Love perceives the universal affectional needs common to humanity and responds with insight from the heart.

Most of us do not grow beyond the controls of our understanding of truth. According to our best thought we accept the laws of order and then try to make our lives measure up. We force ourselves to do what is right. In race relations, most of us, particularly in the beginning, make ourselves act decently because we know that we should. When others look at our actions, it is not easy for them to sort out sincere efforts from put-ons. Even if the actions appear stilted or hard to read, we need to remember that the heart behind self-compulsion is sincere. The truth is that we have a long way to go, but self-compulsion is the only way to really change our focus. God can give us an unselfish heart only if we want Him to and compel ourselves to obey His rules.

But think. If love really guided our lives, there would be no need for arguments for or against quotas defined in civil law. Our civil laws would be just, because as a nation we loved justice. If you have no desire to throw a brick at another, you never think about the law which forbids it.

If we looked on others from genuine love, that love would show us what actions would help others be useful and happy. It would guide us into human decency and moral order. We would not taunt or show disrespect, because the inner and powerful force of affection would say "No." Not Emily Post, or some lesson learned in values clarification, just simple human love would show the way.

Though we have to learn to love, once achieved, love knows how to do what is right without being taught. Those who are happily married do not need to be compelled by civil law to be true for life. A man who loves his wife does not hold her close because moral and social rules say that he should. What is more, if she loves him, even if he is awkward, her heart reaches beyond his awkwardness and she responds from deep within. Because love is our very life, genuine love acts and reacts to the very depth of our humanity. Conscience is not made up of rules. It is the vital force of being useful to others for the very sake of being useful. It is a new will focused not just on others equally with ourselves, but more than ourselves.

This will is new, yet it draws the innocence and trust of infancy to itself. Those golden states of infancy when everything was alive, and we confided fully in those we loved, are renewed. But now because we freely choose them, they become rooted in our very natures. Innocence is no longer ignorant, but informed and even wise.

The rules of fairness we learned in childhood become simply the way we are. Habits, yes, but more than training they are simply the way we act because we have chosen to continue in them. We get along with others simply because we want to.

The reasonable behavior we struggled so hard to work out in youth serves conscience like a loyal and faithful servant. We get respect because we give it.

Inspired by love, the whole story of an individual's spiritual development resolves into one dedicated human being. From that love so painfully acquired, the lessons of the past descend and become the basis, the container, and the support of everything that person stands for. They give his character form, not as lessons anymore, but as ways of expressing who he has truly become.

Because we are free, this world is a mixture of good and evil. It is unrealistic to expect heaven on earth. The opportunity to receive a loving disposition from our God is not a Utopian dream, but a hope which can only be realized individually through our free choices. Universal love is the very life of heaven and eternal life. Heaven itself is no mixture of good and evil. It is a kingdom of mutual love, where genuine humanity can emerge creatively and freely in a life of useful service to our neighbor forever.

Listen to the Babel of the birds on the early morning air. A blanket of voices lifts to the joy of life. Chattering, chuttering, tittering, chuckling here, there, together, alone. Waves of sound rise and fall on the stillness as if nature has an unseen sound equalizer in constant motion. Distinguishable, then not—a solo then a chorus, harmony and dissonance, what does it mean? The "awnk" of the pheasant makes his point. The crow's alarm bursts out, then is gradually lost as he flees his fears. A cardinal demands recognition, then fades in gentle repetition. A nearby house wren quickly bubbles, "This is my home, so precious to me, so precious to me, so precious to me." I know that voice. I feel I must hear each voice, and yet...Now the tractor's voice intrudes, trucks murmur on distant roads, machines grind. Are the earlier sweeter calls still there? Another morning will come.

With one hand I feel worthless—with the other I pray and hope. I long for certainty, yet have the power to destroy it utterly—under-mining its comfort through self-confidence. I think long thoughts of short duration. They seem profound, still I cannot hold them. I want to advise, to reduce pain, to know for sure, but does learning come through sure knowledge? Understanding surges deep within when our whole being cries out for it and yet we admit with finality that only God gives comprehension. Love is our life. It feels so much our own, yet it too is a gift, to treas-ure or to spurn. Even our ability to serve comes from Him alone. All these gifts can come to each of us, unique and measured to our natures. Only in seeing and loving our Maker can we find our humanity.